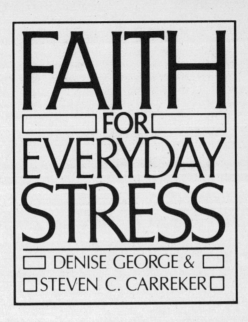

FAITH FOR EVERYDAY STRESS

DENISE GEORGE & STEVEN C. CARREKER

BROADMAN PRESS
Nashville, Tennessee

© Copyright 1988 • Broadman Press
All rights reserved
4250-62
ISBN: 0-8054-5062-9

Dewey Decimal Classification: 157
Subject Heading: STRESS (PSYCHOLOGY)
Library of Congress Catalog Card Number: 88-2839

Printed in the United States of America

Library of Congress Cataloging-in-Publication Data

George, Denise.
  Faith for everyday stress.

  1. Faith. 2. Stress (Psychology) 3. Christian
life. I. Carreker, Steven C.,
1949-   II. Title.
BV4637.G46 1988   248.8'6   88-2839
ISBN 0-8054-5062-9 (pbk.)

FOREWORD

Faith for Everyday Stress by Denise George and Steven Carreker is a brave and helpful book. It sings the gospel note: Life doesn't have to be like this! And it helps us discover how we can change our ways to make life the best it can be.

The book is brave on two fronts. First, it is brave by the personal confessions made here of two lives buffeted by stress. But in our day deluged by personal confessions, it is braver still: Steven and Denise hazard to provide us answers they have found in the midst of their debilitating stresses and to offer them to us. In an age of easy confession and fashionable cynicism, these two have the courage to go beyond confession and give us profound glimpses of what has helped them: the nurturing of an everyday faith.

They help us conquer the killing everydayness of stress. It is probably easier to summon divine help for the extraordinary difficulties of life than for the everyday kind; but, as these two show us, it is the accumulation of everyday stresses that can do us in. So Denise and Steven provide us a much-needed book, a resource for meeting everyday stresses with an everyday faith.

They offer us in readable form some of the best, most current research on stress. They help us identify what stress is doing in our lives. Stress and fatigue are insidious in that they are invisible; they hide themselves from our awareness often until they have begun to do obvious damage. This book helps us discern early warning signals. And it provides several "self-help" questionnaires that enable us to identify our particular stresses and stressors. I found myself saying "that's me" over and over.

But as I have mentioned, they go far beyond confession and diagnosis to prescription, the offering of profound spiritual guidance, prescriptions for health: bodily, mental, and spiritual. I found their guidance to be clear and sure. The last section of the book is a practical case-study approach that proves its everyday usefulness.

Killing stress is a combination of significant external stresses and inadequate personal resources with which to meet these stresses. Neglected in much of the current literature on stress, technical and popular, is the guidance in finding *spiritual* resources for coping. Yet such guidance is crucial on two counts. First of all, how we meet life with meaning, understanding, and hope determines to a large degree how well we survive. Religious wisdom and values are a crucial resource for meeting life's stresses, and our authors lead us well. Secondly, God's own Spirit is Himself the *power of blessing* which is the daily, continuous life-force that heals and renews and bestows a sense of well-being. When our human spirit opens itself to the Spirit of God, we receive the everyday miracle of health. Such is a dimension of God's power of salvation, the power unto health. God wishes that for you, and this book helps you become partners with God toward your health and well-being.

I read this book during a particularly stressful time in my life. I was moved by the personal confessions of stress illness and by the testimony of their recoveries toward health. I found myself edified by their wise guidance. And as a pastor, I was given a new resource in my ministry to others. It helped God minister to me and now enhances my ministry to others. I will hand this book to people who come to me overwhelmed by life's stresses.

Denise, a gifted laywoman with a vocation as a writer, and Steven, an accomplished pastor, have written a book I am honored and pleased to introduce. They live courageously, they write clearly with wisdom and humor, and they seek to walk with the God of health and blessing. Reading this book helps us on our way.

H. STEPHEN SHOEMAKER
Louisville, Kentucky

ACKNOWLEDGMENT I

There are always so many people to thank when one writes a book. There are those who inspire, those who encourage, those who support, and those who give rolled-up-sleeve practical help.

"Thank you" seems too inadequate a word for those people closest to me. Nevertheless, I know of no other word to convey my deepest feelings of indebtedness and gratitude.

So I say thank you, Timothy, for your constant words of support and encouragement, and for your eighteen years of dedicated and faithful covenant love. I am deeply grateful to you and deeply thankful to God for you. You make it possible for me to write.

Thank you, Christian and Alyce, for being thoughtful and considerate children who understand and celebrate your mother's strong dedication to ministry through the written word.

Thank you, Steve Shoemaker, for being my pastor and my friend, and for taking valuable time to read and to make much-needed suggestions on this manuscript.

Thank you, Dr. Wayne Oates, teacher and friend, for introducing me to the study of stress and crisis management through your classes at The Southern Baptist Theological Seminary and through your numerous books on the subject.

Thank you, Terry Helwig, Helen Parker, Jim Cox, Lucien Coleman, and Sue Kidd for being special "writer-friends" to me, for your encouragement, support, and unending enthusiasm.

Thank you, Anna Katherine Pierson, who, through your continued help, enables me to write.

I also wish to thank two institutions who hold great meaning in my life: Southern Baptist Theological Seminary and Crescent Hill Baptist Church.

And, to you, my good parents, Bob and Willene Wyse, who stay close to me in all my pursuits, a special word of thanks.

I am indebted to all of you who continue to teach me, inspire me, encourage me, and lead me toward greater understanding.

DENISE GEORGE
Louisville, Kentucky
Autumn 1987

ACKNOWLEDGMENT II

I am indebted to Wayne Dyer, mentor of the early 1970s, who convinced me that one need not accept self-defeating behaviors as a way of life. He taught me that one could do something about enriching life. He put psychology into specifics.

I acknowledge the covenant between me and First Baptist Church, Boone, in which we allow each other room for honest struggle and support of encouragement and prayer.

I am most indebted to and thankful for my family of Sherri, Kirstin, and Sophia. Their support formed the incubator of survival in stressful days and the party of faith celebration in the days that followed.

Steven C. Carreker
Boone, North Carolina
Autumn 1987

Contents

Section I
Denise's Story
of Stress and Faith

For whatever is born of God
overcomes the world;
and this is the victory
that overcomes the world,
our faith.

1 John 5:4

1
A Plane Destined to Crash

Late one night, as I lay in bed exhausted and in terrible physical pain, I prayed the most selfish prayer a mother of two young children could ever pray.

"Lord," I whispered softly so no one could hear me. "I can no longer deal with the heavy demands in my life. Please, please, Lord, just let me die tonight in my sleep so I can find some rest."

It was the first real prayer I had prayed in a long time.

Stress, caused by a terrific work load as well as mental, emotional, and physical pain, plus exhaustion, had finally claimed me as its victim. The everydayness of the everyday, combined with some hard-hitting crises, had become too much for me to handle. I needed relief from it all, and I prayed that the ultimate relief would come.

The crises had happened all at once and had caught me off my guard. They came, not as a farmer would carefully space his seeds to give ample growing room, but as his young son would playfully dump the whole packet of seeds into the first newly dug hole. I had no growing room between the crises, no space for insightful contemplation. I couldn't get back up on my feet after one hard blow until another came and knocked me down again.

During those long days, God and I had become somewhat distant. We didn't talk much anymore. I had become far too busy to give Him much time. And, to be honest, I believe I felt angry with God. If He loved me as much as He promised, then why would He distance Himself just when I needed Him most?

Where was God within the tight space of five years, when I experienced severe crises of sickness, surgery, new and overwhelming responsibilities, homesickness, loneliness, and the loss of two people I dearly loved? During those five years, I felt as if I was thrashing around on the surface of the sea, trying hard just to keep my head above water.

Stress had now replaced God as my constant companion.

The Crises

I had waited some eleven years to become pregnant with my first child. It was an experience I had prayed for and longed for. The pregnancy, however, did not go smoothly. I was almost completely bedridden for the first four months with severe nausea and dehydration. There were also complications with a natural delivery, so my son came into the world by emergency cesarean section, surgery I had not anticipated, surgery that had frightened me. I would spend many months trying to fully recover from it.

When my son, Christian, was only fifteen months old, I became pregnant a second time. We were thrilled with the planned pregnancy, but the first trimester of pregnancy proved even more difficult than the first time around. I spent weeks in the hospital, and we worried we would lose our unborn daughter.

Daughter Alyce also came by cesarean section. Once I was home, with almost full responsibility for a newborn baby and an active toddler, my recovery from the surgery proved painfully slow with many repeatedly pulled incision muscles.

During those days of sickness, surgery, and slow recuperation, I wondered if I would survive. The childhood faith that had been nurtured in me over a lifetime by two loving parents and grandparents, which had sustained me up to now, seemed lost somewhere in all the confusion I felt. I almost stopped going to church. I stopped reading and studying the Scriptures. And I almost stopped praying. I tried hard to keep a smile on my face for my own small world to see, but inside I felt alone, troubled, and sad.

Needless to say, parenting two children under two years of age overwhelmed me. I barely had time to brush my hair. Day after day, I had no break from the awesome and demanding job of mothering. Instant parenting! No experience. No enclosed directions. If someone had hit me smack in the face with a Louisville Slugger, I don't think the shock would have been as great!

I can remember sitting in the dentist's chair one morning having my teeth cleaned. The dental assistant busily scraped and dug her instruments around and between my teeth. Before I had children, I would have dreaded an hour at the dentist's. But as a new mother, so physically depleted of energy, I actually enjoyed the change, a sort of minivacation, even if in the dentist's chair!

In the midst of having babies and having surgery, and before I had had a chance to even begin to cope with these day-to-day stresses, I had to deal with other painful crises that would buckle my knees.

First, my beloved grandmother died only a few days before my daughter, Alyce, her only namesake, was born. Since my husband, Timothy, was asked to preach her funeral, I spent the weekend at home with only a two-year-old to comfort me. I sat for two days in my yellow porch swing in intense August heat, feeling angry with God for what I then considered cruel timing, and crying because I was too far along in the pregnancy to travel to her funeral. I was never able to tell her good-bye.

Less than three years after I lost my grandmother, my grandfather died unexpectedly one night in his sleep. I felt as if I had been standing on a carpet one minute, and the next minute the carpet had been jerked out from under me. Just when I needed them most, my grandparents—my spiritual nurturers—were gone. I still had my parents, but they lived three hundred miles away.

And, believe it or not, along came more stress. Somewhere between my babies becoming toddlers and my grandparents' deaths, as I struggled just to catch my daily breath, yet another crisis came.

Since Timothy had taught church history for seven years at The Southern Baptist Theological Seminary in Louisville, Kentucky, he was due a teaching sabbatical. The seminary required him to go away for one year to do research and writing in his field of study. So, his area of study being John Calvin in Geneva, we rented out our house, our car, and our cat, stuffed a year's worth of clothing into the airline's maximum seven suitcases, and flew off to Switzerland for a year.

Now flying to Switzerland for a year seemed like a dream to me at first; but after arriving, I found the day-to-day stress on me there almost unbearable. We lived in a tiny, cramped apartment. I couldn't speak or understand the Swiss-German language. I knew few people. And even simple tasks like grocery shopping or banking or driving proved extremely difficult. I painfully missed my family in Chattanooga, as well as my friends back home in Louisville. Since Timothy had to spend most of his time researching and traveling throughout Switzerland, Germany, Yugoslavia, and Hungary, I mothered almost single-handedly two small preschoolers who had not yet been potty trained.

Never in my life had I been so homesick or so lonely. The redeeming light of that year, however, came through the love and presence of some special friends we made while there. But, on the whole, the everyday stresses of living in a foreign country crowded my thoughts and destroyed my sense of upcoming hope. I allowed that stress to so bog me down that I seemed to lose touch with God. Even among the majestic Alps, the tall snow-tipped pines, and the turquoise lakes, the God who was closer than breathing and "nearer than hands and feet"—the God that Tennyson so beautifully praised in pen—seemed nowhere to be found. Daily stress and exhausting work seemed to devour my spirituality bit by bit.

The Turning Point

Every story has its turning point. It is that almost indescribable, life-changing point when something happens, if only for a second, to lift the veil that shadows our souls.

And so it was for me.

My turning point came in the form of severe physical pain. My body was tired, exhausted, and filled with more stress than it could physically bear. Then, not unexpectedly, the dam broke. I felt as if I could no longer keep my head above water. I was finally drowning, tired of fighting the waves. My descent to the bottom of the sea had begun.

The daily stress, the tension I wrestled with hourly, and the fatigue turned on its own body. I developed a condition known as Myofascial Pain Dysfunction Syndrome (MPD for short), a chronic degenerative disease affecting the jaw joint and, in my case, caused by a nighttime unconscious grinding of the teeth in unreleased stress.

The pain in my jaw grew constant and, at times, unbearable. Without warning, sharp wrenching pain would shoot into my face and head, down into my neck, shoulders, and back. Treatment after expensive treatment, I saw no change in my condition. I was only getting worse.

"You've got to find some relief from all this stress," my doctor told me again and again.

But I could find no relief, no resting place from it. I had small active children, a busy husband, a house to clean, bills to pay, laundry, shopping—a great mass of responsibility that continually called out to me, needed me. On top of home responsibilities, as a writer and author, I had book and article and speech deadlines to meet. Where was I to find rest?

To make matters worse, the specialist also discovered I had a large amount of unexpected bone breakdown and muscle damage in my jaw joint. And he found that the MPD problem had begun to affect my right jaw joint as well. It hurt to talk or to chew my food. My doctor prescribed large dosages of muscle relaxers and painkillers that I took around the clock.

But not even the painkillers could kill the pain I felt. Nothing seemed to work. Finally I gave up the battle. Stress had won. It had done its damage. I thought I would never be free from pain, both inside and outside, again.

* * *

This is my story of everyday unreleased stress. Daily stress and pain made me want to give up. I could no longer live with it. It had a grip on me that I couldn't seem to shake.

During those five years, I had tried to control my own life. I thought I could handle the everyday crises and stresses all by myself. I saw myself as the sole pilot of my own plane, "pulling myself up by my own bootstraps," trying to be strong enough to cope with anything that might fall into my cluttered path. Looking back, I can now see that I piloted a plane destined to crash.

Fortunately, however, my story is not over.

2
Coming Home Again

I lay in bed late that unforgettable night, my jaw hot with blinding pain, and I prayed. Never before had my prayer been so intense. I wanted to die just like my grandfather had died, passing gently into sleep. I couldn't control the pressures in my life anymore, the stresses I faced every day. Giving up seemed easier, my last hope for rest.

The major crises, one stacked upon another, had confused and frustrated me. Day-to-day life was just too hard. I felt tired. I could not emotionally digest all the drastic changes. With my babies' births and my grandparents' deaths, life and death had rubbed shoulders, and I could not cope with it all. My life seemed grossly out of control, within and without.

Although the big crises hit me hard, I now believe they were probably less stress producing than the everyday ordinary frustrations I felt. The exhaustion of parenting, the deep sense of loss, the lack of hope, and the great distance I felt from God caused me considerable stress.

At thirty-five years of age, I lay in my bed feeling too discouraged to go on. Little did I know, however, that that prayer would begin to change the course of my life.

The Dream

Perhaps it was only a dream that followed my prayer. But, quite to my surprise, as I lay there, I began to feel an unex-

23

pected sense of warmth and well-being. A kind of peace began to slowly encircle me like the strong nurturing arms of a loved one. I found myself thinking back to my childhood, back to the restful and delightful summers I spent on my grandparents' farm.

In my thoughts, I sat with Papa early one evening on the dark brown living-room couch, Bible in his hand, and listened to him ask me about my life. "Do you want to live your life for Jesus, 'Nisey?" he questioned, his sky-blue eyes searching my young round face.

My answer came quickly. "Yes, Papa, I do." Even at such a tender age, I had long felt and seen God's love through the nurture and example of my grandparents. Papa and I prayed for a long time together in thanksgiving over my new faith decision. I rejoiced. I was coming home to God.

My dream continued. As if in slow motion, I walked with Papa through his vegetable garden and with Mama through her flower bed. The freshly mowed yard, the large white frame house, the tall hickory nut tree—they were all the same. As beautiful to me as the day I had been brought there to live with my parents as a three-day-old baby. Nothing had changed.

Inside the house, I noticed the family Bible that always lay opened on the table. Surrounding it were letters and thoughtful cards from Mama's many friends. Papa's brightly colored Scripture-verse cards sat upright in a plastic loaf of "daily bread" on the kitchen counter. They had become quite faded, as we had read them again and again before each meal. Papa's "instruments of praise"—an old guitar and a spinet piano—stood back in the corner of the hallway.

As I glanced around the room, I saw Papa sitting quietly, eyes closed, head back in his favorite fabric-worn chair, a chair I called his "meditation chair." I knew he was praying.

Through the window I could see Mama, her small body weak and frail from a lifetime of sickness, as she continued her walk through the flower bed, reaching down to touch each remembered rose, her lips moving in silent praise.

For a long moment, I held onto the sight of the smiling eyes and softly lined faces of my grandparents: peaceful, contented, and truly happy faces. I watched them as they moved gracefully about their day. An inner beauty followed them and reflected onto every word they said, every note they sang, and everything they touched. They, too, knew about sickness, surgery, loss, homesickness, loneliness, and exhaustion. Yet they coped. They filled their days with unceasing prayer, praise, gratitude, and abundant love for God, family, friends, and beyond.

A New Morning

Too soon, my night ended. I woke early that morning, and I held tightly to the glow of the night's dream. I felt I had once again entered my grandparents' world, a world of unconditional love and acceptance, of freedom, and of delightful rest. I felt I had come home, if only in a dream, to the farm of my childhood and to the faith I had learned and loved as a child. And, somehow, I now felt vaguely different.

The dream was a turning point for me.

I wish I could tell you that during the night God snapped His fingers, instantly healed my painful jaw, and miraculously changed my life. I wish I could tell you that in an overnight flash, He took away all the everyday stresses that weighed so heavily on me.

But I can't.

Although it was a "new" morning, I once again woke up to a house that needed cleaning, to laundry that shouted to be sorted, to writing deadlines that refused to wait, and to two children who were still not potty trained.

Change did not happen in a flash, but, upon waking, I knew I had found an answer. I had been given a journey back in time, and I had again seen the beauty and quality of my grandparents' faith.

That night I discovered their secret of faith. It was an answer to my prayer. Simple, yet profound. My grandparents had an *everyday faith*, one that balanced the everyday stresses and pressures they felt, one that followed them throughout their day and gave them relief.

I didn't really understand what was happening to me, but, at any rate, with my eyes now more widely open, I felt I would no longer need to fight quite as hard to keep my head above the waves. Perhaps God was calling me to a sort of second-childhood faith.

Over the next new weeks, I began to see how very different my grandparents' faith was from mine. *They had an everyday faith; I had a once-in-a-while faith.* They had a faith that reached out and grabbed every hour with joy and gratitude. I had a faith that had forgotten how to worship, that opened a Bible only randomly, and that cried out in prayer only when in desperation.

Needless to say, the months that followed proved life changing for me. I traveled back often in my thoughts to my grandparents' farm, and I "studied" with renewed interest my grandparent's faith. I decided I no longer wanted a once-in-a-while faith. I wanted my grandparents' hour-to-hour faith. Since that decision, a decision not unlike the one I made while sitting on the dark brown living-room couch with my grandfather,

I've Made Some Fascinating Discoveries

I once read Marion Bond West's story of her husband's long illness and death. She, too, struggled with unlimited stress, deep grief, and discouragement. Often she felt she was "drowning in icy waters of fear."[1] Something remarkable happened to her, however. Her turning point came, too.

She imagined that God smiled and told her to keep swimming until she reached an island: the Island of Trust. She listened; then one day she gave up her struggle and climbed onto the Island. She began to trust God day by day until she no longer felt afraid. Once on the Island, she found the needed strength to endure the stress of her husband's terminal illness. Daily hugging the shore, she began to move closer and closer to God. She finally came to the point that, even as death overshadowed her husband, she no longer feared what was happening but found peace and restful sleep.

I, too, have begun my climb onto Marion's Island, the Island of everyday faith and trust in the One who has promised me rest. I needed to come home again to God and to reclaim the roots of my childhood faith.

I had been like the prodigal son who left the Father for a while and tried to make it on his own. I, too, couldn't survive in the far country. I wanted to come home again, to live out my everydays in my Father's home of unconditional love, acceptance, freedom, and delightful rest. I feel I am now walking down the long road toward home, finally coming back to the One who has waited so long to run and greet me.

The Homecoming

My everydays have been in the process of changing since I decided to come back to the Father. Constantly calling to memory my grandparents' faith, I have been actively seeking an hour-to-hour closeness to God: an everyday faith. I wanted to once again feel whole, to live a life with meaning.

My pastor, Stephen Shoemaker, puts it this way: "When we by faith say our 'yes' back to God, we are moved into a relationship with God that brings us wholeness, meaning, and confidence."[2]

I wanted that kind of faith, that kind of close relationship with God.

The decision to change a long-practiced life-style is never an easy one. But I knew if I wanted faith to move up to the front seat of my life, and stress to move to the backseat, I would have to make some drastic changes.

I didn't jump into full-fledged everyday faith overnight, but little by little, day by day, I prayed for guidance, and I began to purposely change my daily routine.

I.

I surmised that if I wanted my life to become God-centered instead of stress-centered, if I wanted God to "Create in me a clean heart, . . ./and put a new and right spirit within me" (Ps. 51:10), I would need to spend more time with God. So (quite reluctantly at first) I began to rise an hour earlier in the mornings to pray and to listen. That would at least be a beginning, I thought.

On more mornings than I care to admit, however, I pulled the warm blankets over my head and drifted back to sleep. But in time, rising early became routine. I now look forward to this morning hour, to sit alone in the darkened den while my family sleeps, and to pray until the sun barely lightens the dawning sky. I find Him during this hour, the One who has promised to be "near to all who call upon him" (Ps.

145:18). This time of quiet communion sets my whole day on the right course.

II.

Since I felt my life had not been in good order, and that that alone had caused unusual stress, I wrote up a list of priorities—not what my priorities *had* been but what I *wanted* them to be. I discovered I gave far too much time, energy, and thought to my writing career and not nearly enough to my family. And I had given God far too little time. My new list began with God first, family and friends second, career third, and so on.

Putting "career" so far down on my priority list wasn't easy for me. I had clearly felt God's call to a writing and speaking ministry, and I had an overly ambitious desire to write and publish. Yet, at that point, I felt God had issued to me an even stronger call and commitment to my family and friends. Reaching out to them in love and self-giving was also my ministry for Him.

Knowing my priorities (*and* taping the list to my refrigerator door within almost constant view) helped me to make better decisions about how I would spend my days. And that cut down on a considerable amount of unnecessary stress.

III.

I also began to pray for daily forgiveness. "Forgive us our debts,/As we also have forgiven our debtors" (Matt. 6:12), Jesus taught us to pray. Being human, I knew that inside each day I committed sin, either in thought or deed. I needed daily forgiveness for that plain, old-fashioned, hard-to-hear word *sin,* for I "missed the mark" many times during my daily walk with God.

As a highly sensitive person whose stomach churns when

an evil thought even comes to mind, I had long felt the keen, stinging, and largely unforgiven sins piling up inside me. I dragged behind me a long, heavy chain of sin-stress. It had weighed me down and kept me from becoming all I could become in Christ. I wanted to come clean, for I couldn't live with unresolved sin in my life.

I knew I needed *daily* forgiveness. So, before going to sleep at night, I began to confess these sins to God. And He forgave me. I began to ask forgiveness from others I had wronged, and I forgave those who had wronged or hurt me. I also began to forgive myself.

The stress of sin disappeared. Forgiving and forgiven, I could live more peaceably with myself, my *forgiving* and *forgiven* self. The fierce inner battles of conflict and turmoil ceased to rage within me. My stomach stopped churning. The following mornings, I could wake up free from the stress of unresolved and unforgiven sin. And it felt so good!

IV.

I began to read my Bible again. Moved it down from the bookcase to the kitchen table, within easy reach. I remembered that, not long before his death, Papa decided to read the entire Bible again. He had read it many times before. He had read it enthusiastically, forever stopping and underlining God's promises, even setting music to favorite verses. He finished the last page of his Bible only a few days before he died.

Why not? I picked up my Bible, blew off the dust, and started at page 1. I now read every day, even if only a few chapters. As I read, I am sensing and understanding Papa's rare enthusiasm over God's written Word. I can hold God's promises close in mind throughout the day. Whenever the day's stresses become too much for me, I can find continuing reassurance and hope in His Word.

V.

In my plan for more ways to become "everyday faithful," I chose "meditation chairs" throughout my home where I could often take a moment's spiritual rest. During the day, especially when feeling too stressed, I would head for one of my chairs. I would lean back, close my eyes, think of God, and rest in Him. My muscles relaxed, my heart beating slower, my mind clearer, I could then return to my day feeling much less stressed.

VI.

Daily walks have been a pleasurable part of my new routine. Before, I would not have allowed the time and energy for walking my neighborhood in circles. It accomplished nothing, I thought.

Was I ever wrong! Since, I've found that walking several miles briskly by myself at least once a day opens channels for communication with God that I've never before experienced. (Perhaps the legs, heart, and mind are somehow uniquely intertwined!) I walk and get good tension-releasing exercise. I walk and my heart pours out in prayer, confession, thanksgiving, and praise to God. I walk and I hear God's whisper as it fills my mind with new insights into life and faith. Walking has become so important to me that I could not go one day without it.

VII.

I decided to be nicer to—and more tolerant with—my husband and children. When frustrated or angry with them, I now stop and pray for ten seconds before I speak. My words come out softer, more understanding, and more loving this way.

I am trying to listen more intently to—and really hear—what my husband and children tell me. And they are talking more now. Communication with them has become more honest and open and loving. We enjoy spending more time together, taking more evening walks, holding hands and praying regularly, snuggling with each other and toasting marshmallows around the family room fireplace. Oh, we still have our disagreements, for they are inevitable in family relationship. But they are quieter now, far less stressful, and more quickly put behind us, forgiven and forgotten.

VIII.

I am praying more now, for family, friends, strangers I pass in the malls, and the world's people in general. I am seeing many of these prayers answered.

" 'Nisey, we call your name *every day* in prayer." I smile as I recall Mama and Papa's words to me. How comforting those words were, to know someone prayed daily for me. I now tell that good news to my children, husband, family, and friends. "I call your name every day in prayer." To my unexpected joy, as my children hear my words and watch my new everyday expressions of faith, they, too, are picking up good faithful habits, habits that one day will save them from front-seat stress.

IX.

I have begun to choose my stress-causing battles more carefully. I now *decide* what issues I will allow to receive stress, and how much stress. So what if Alyce wants to wear her winter velveteen party dress to Sunday School in the middle of August! Why become deadlocked in battle over the attire of a four-year-old when, all things considered, it really doesn't matter? Now if Alyce decides to ride her Hot Cycle in the middle of Clipping Cross Road, that's a legitimate battle. I would choose to be more stressful over that one. But by keeping to my priorities and by carefully choosing what I will allow to stress me, I now have more control over daily stress.

X.

With each passing day, as I work harder toward living an everyday faith, I'm striving to find other ways to be more faithful.

Jesus said, "Love one another" (John 13:34). I am trying to do that by providing a listening ear for friends who need to talk, writing more notes of encouragement, and praying and working harder for those around the world who hurt. Each day brings its own share of opportunities to reach out in love.

I have also found my place back in my church. In my doubt and despair, I had stopped attending regularly. I've come to dearly love Crescent Hill Baptist Church. I am now involved in Sunday School. I eagerly anticipate each worship, preaching, and teaching service. And I am seeking to find more ways to reach out with my gifts to my church in ministry.

I have also begun to ask God for career guidance, insight, and energy to meet writing and speaking demands. All in all, I am laughing more, hugging more, and am, generally, loving people more. I'm struggling to become more childlike, to more honestly face my doubts, to worry less about the future, and to trust God more in the present. I am trying to step back from myself to give God complete control of all my minutes. I am praying to become more open, more giving, and more vulnerable to my family, friends, and others. During the minutes of my everyday, I am striving to be less "Denise-centered" and more Christ-centered.

This hasn't been easy for me. As you might expect, I'm not *there* yet. I often fall off my Island and slip back into the deep icy waters. I still have some lonely, exhausting, and just plain stressful days.

But I'm trying.

And I am finding the moments of my daily routine somehow transformed, changed. Oh, I still have meals to cook, children to chauffeur, clothes to fold, school meetings to attend, and writing deadlines to meet. But I now spend my time much differently than I did. For I am trying hard to model my minutes after my grandparents' minutes, striving to fill my days with unceasing prayer, praise, gratitude, and abundant love for God, family, friends, and beyond.

The Results

I am finding that as my daily faith grows, my daily stress is becoming drastically reduced. And the inevitable stress I must cope with no longer discourages me as much as it once did.

Remarkably, and to my grateful surprise, within weeks of my faith decision, I could stop taking the painkillers for my jaw. I no longer needed them. The pain in my jaw began to diminish day by day until, within a few months, I no longer needed the specialist or his expensive treatments. I am still amazed at this.

What happened? I believe with the psalmist that "the Lord is near to the brokenhearted, and saves the crushed in spirit" (Ps. 34:18). I had been brokenhearted and crushed in spirit by my under-used faith and by my overwhelming stress. The Lord truly came near to me the night I wanted to give up. I can't really explain it; but I believe that, because of my new relationship with God, the pain on the inside of me began to fade, and the pain on the outside faded as well. Now, a year and a half later, I have no more pain or jaw problem at all.

My new "second-childhood faith" is exciting to me. Each day brings its own faith discoveries and adventures. I believe I am finally discovering a bit of Papa and Mama's *everyday faith*. And I am finding it to be a faith that is strong enough to stand up to the daily stresses that threaten to knock me down. I am in awe of this faith, a bottomless well of faith I never knew existed, a daily faith I can live with, live for, and can no longer live without.

My journey into faith, however, is just beginning. What I have discovered is just the chip of sparkle at the tip of the iceberg. Yet, already, I am feeling the closeness with God that Tennyson found so many years ago, a closeness that brings with it the gift of peace, contentment, and happiness. Once again I am discovering the wholeness, meaning, and confidence that comes with hour-to-hour faith in Jesus Christ.

And I no longer want to be sole pilot of my own plane.

Where was God within the tight space of five years when I experienced almost overwhelming crises and everyday stresses? I know now that He was right beside me, running to offer me an Island to climb upon and find rest. In that discovery, I now rejoice. For I am coming home to God again.

* * *

I pray that my story of stress and my story of faith's journey has somehow touched a note in you. I have tried to be as open and as honest as I can be. It is difficult for me to make myself so vulnerable to you; but it is my hope that in doing so, you can in some way relate to my story and find faith and strength and hope for your own journey.

Notes

1. Marion Bond West, *The Nevertheless Principle* (Old Tappan, N.J.: Fleming H. Revell Co., 1986), p. 75.

2. H. Stephen Shoemaker, *The Jekyll and Hyde Syndrome* (Nashville: Broadman Press, 1987), p. 161.

Section II
Steven's Story
of Stress and Faith

We are afflicted in every way, but not crushed;
perplexed, but not driven to despair;
persecuted, but not forsaken;
struck down, but not destroyed. . . .
So we do not lose heart.

2 Corinthians 4:8-9,16

3
Imprisoned by Everyday Stress

"You have a small ulcer on the right side of your stomach, Steven," my doctor confirmed. "It is not malignant. I repeat, it is *not* malignant."

After a week of unusual abdominal pain, and after hours of tests and X rays, I had waited for what seemed years for that telephone call.

"Malignant?" I had never associated "malignant" with an ulcer. Actually, I hadn't given much thought to an ulcer. And I never thought I would have one.

Malignancy? Cancer? How close was I to this dreadful disease? Suddenly my stomach pain left, and a light-headed feeling of fear and anxiety overcame me. Was the doctor sure? How could I be assured this ulcer could be relieved and that there was no malignancy?

I headed toward the drugstore for a prescription to start the healing process. But I stopped two miles from home. I felt too faint-headed to drive. Nauseated with fear, I was overwhelmed. My otherwise healthy life had been abruptly interrupted with illness.

Somehow I regained composure and returned home. I phoned my wife, told her the news, and asked her to pick up the prescription. I will never forget her angry response.

"An ulcer? You told me you never worried. I can't believe this! How could you have an ulcer?"

Though we later agreed her anger was a first-burst expression of fear for me, I used her response to push me into some difficult questions. Did I worry? Was I uptight? Did I have something knotted or bottled up inside me? What caused the ulcer? Stress? Was my anxiety actually cutting a hole in my stomach? Even though I knew that one couldn't be sure of the exact causes of ulcers, the pain and fear were real enough to make me do whatever was necessary to regain my health.

I knew the right questions to ask myself. I had been scheduled to lead a stress relief conference at Ridgecrest, North Carolina! During this time I was working long hours to prepare for it. It is true that you best teach what you need to learn. I was familiar with all the academia of stress: psychological growth stages, faith development thoughts, the description of self-actualizing and self-defeating behavior. I was a counselor and pastor who listened and responded to people undergoing unusual stress. Yes, I knew the questions. It was not easy, however, asking them of myself.

It did not take long for me to ask and answer my questions and to group my stressors. They included a recent move, family concerns, my job, and an abnormal amount of grief.

Moving and Geographical Rootlessness

During the months prior to the discovery of my ulcer, I felt geographically unattached. I could say with Wesley, "The world is my parish." The world might have been my parish, but I felt I had nowhere in the world to call home. I wanted a place of intimacy and rest. A home would offer me a sense of temporary permanence, and I did not feel I had that. We wanted to feel at home in our recent move to Boone, North Carolina, where I had accepted the position of church pastor. But nonetheless we felt unsettled. We were renting a house, and despite how nice it was, we kept thinking we would move to a permanent home the next month, or perhaps the next.

Moving to Boone also caused our daughters, Kirstin and Sophia, much stress. New teachers and new places were nice, but as the "new kids," they felt the silent exclusion of the "in-crowds."

Typical stress followed our move, things like turning on electricity and water, locating trash pickups, unpacking boxes, connecting the washer and dryer. As long as six months after the move, we still felt as though we were moving.

Family: In Search of Time Together

I have a strong wife, Sherri, and we are blessed with two strong-willed daughters, Kirstin and Sophia. We are open and honest with each other. We talk things over. We offer mutual nurturance.

With four strong-willed, independent-thinking people in our family, we each do our own thing. We enjoy the financial and self-esteem benefits of being a two-paycheck family. But we also know the price: too little time together. We live together in the same house, yet we are hardly ever there together.

At the time of my ulcer, family support was strong, but family time was stretched. Geographical separation from grandparents and relatives had always been stressful for us. Lack of family time was a growing ache. We rode around in the same car, but we seldom went to the same place. We allowed too many people to pull on us.

In ulcer pain, more than ever, I wanted to relieve the stress of missing my family. I wanted them. I needed them. I needed to know they also wanted and needed me. I wanted more family time together.

Vocation: A Job Never Finished

I traveled daily to my job with an old, worn-out briefcase. In reflection, I called it my "Linus blanket." I had carried this briefcase through seminary and two other pastorates. By now, it felt comfortable in more ways than one.

Comfortable to the touch and worn with the weight of books and use, the briefcase felt soft, flexible, and familiar to the shape of my shoulder. It looked pathetic, however, and was ready to fall apart.

It was also comfortable to my mind and self-esteem. Somehow, it gave me the daily assurance that I was working hard to do the job of pastor. It told me I was a hard worker, eager to do whatever was needed to get the job done.

But my briefcase, my "Linus blanket," covered up some real anxiety.

I have learned that the work of a pastor is never finished. The briefcase covered up my anxiety over this sense of incompleteness. I could never quite finish a sermon or all the visits or all the administration. I did not like living with incompleteness. I had been taught to finish my work. I knew that until I learned to live with incompleteness, my Linus blanket briefcase was necessary.

But even a Linus blanket couldn't cover up an overly stressed stomach. I burned the candle at both ends. I made list after list of things not completed. I drank cup after cup of coffee, always thinking one more surge of caffeine would throw me over the top of the incompleted pile of tasks at hand.

My Linus blanket also covered up my anxiety of external role expectations placed on me as pastor. Our congregation is diverse. While one person expected high-powered evangelistic preaching, another preferred a gentle announcement of grace. I did not like being disliked by either group, and this proved painful for me. Role expectations were forever making my daily attempt at managing my time seem totally inadequate in view of all the demands placed on me as pastor.

My Linus blanket was also an attempt to cover up my great anxiety of feeling lonely. Loneliness seemed to be my most frequent companion. I felt so sought after, yet so alone. Much of what I did I had to do alone. I prayed alone, visited alone, studied alone. I had to carry the burdens and confessions of my congregation alone. I felt lonely as I made difficult, unpopular decisions in a popularity-driven world. Loneliness seemed to be everywhere.

I do not necessarily believe that aloneness gives birth to loneliness. But aloneness, accumulated task after task, day after day, seemed to call loneliness into full existence. Loneliness seemed the thin wall through which stress penetrated.

Not only did the job stressors of incompleteness, external role expectations, and loneliness place undue stress on me; I often wondered if I was where God wanted me to be. Was I doing what He wanted me to do, and how could I be sure? Loneliness led me to the task and stress of call clarification.

I had been quite content in Asheville, in an inner-city ministry. I did not aspire to a First Baptist pastorate in a county-seat town. I seemed to have entirely different gifts of ministry than most pastors. I had felt that I was doing God's will in moving to Boone. But now, my ulcerated stomach made me wonder.

Grief Had Become My Constant Companion

I walked often with grieving people in my congregations. I suffered with them. I experienced the great sorrow of burying the loved and attended, as well as the unloved and unattended. Our mutual grief had worn on me as I looked into the firm, hollow eyes of weeping survivors.

Grief had been predominant in my move to Boone. I had my own grief, the grief of leaving and letting go of the people I loved and who loved me. The move separated us from significant soul mates, from a church we loved, and from a guardian daughter who had been a rich blessing in our lives. Soul vacancy is often the chamber of grief. I let go of ministries that were necessary for others and, therefore, dear to me. I had been the birthing parent of them. I still could remember the labor pains. Was I abandoning them prematurely? To leave those persons I believed in was to deprive myself of their companionship and to grieve their absence.

My grief, however, seemed no equal to that of my new congregation. Their pastor, my immediate predecessor, had died an early death with cancer only eleven months before my arrival. The church had loved him dearly. He had baptized them, performed their weddings, officiated their funerals, and watched their children grow up. Now he was gone.

To add to the grief, only one month before I began our joint ministry, the church's minister of music had died unexpectedly with a heart attack. Now the other voice of worship was silenced.

Within the first month of our joint ministry, an entry in my journal read, "Eleven days and three funerals. How much grief can we bear?"

Our uncommon grief bonded us in covenant. Exhausted with grief, we constantly had loss on the agenda of our hearts, but this was too infrequently discussed in meetings agenda. We were speechless about this constant companion. We ached, but we did not know what to say. I went to Boone with a ministry call of gentleness, comfort, and healing. Yet my very presence was a reminder of their painful loss.

In the midst of our common grief, I suffered the most profound ache of grief in the death of my maternal grandmother. She and I had bid farewell six months before her death. But still the grief swelled. She was clearly the ancestor of my spiritual lineage. More than any other, I reflected her soul and spirit. And, added to my grief, during her funeral days I frequently recalled the death of our infant daughter.

One last dose of grief I experienced during this time was anticipatory grief. For eight months I had sat with a special friend as her husband died with cancer. He had been my age, and the first symptom of his illness had been stomach pain.

It was a month after Grandmother's death, and only days before my friend's death, that my ulcer exploded into pain. The grief had to get out somehow. In reflection, whatever other stressors went into the potpourri of my ulcer, grief was in the middle.

Was the ulcer malignant? Was I going to die? Now a new question arose. No longer did I ask, "Does stress cause ulcers?" I now asked, "How do I deal with the stress an ulcer causes?"

In Retrospect

Looking back, I see that my stress revisited was a painful journey of a soul in search of becoming, again, what my Creator would have me to be. The truth hurt. It made me feel ashamed, embarrassed, foolish, and stupid. It made me confessional. It made me repentant. So in the long run, though it hurt, the truth helped and brought healing.

My stress revisited taught me I had no claim to uniqueness in the stress category. I realized that moving, family, job, and grief were common stress experiences. They were everyday stresses. Every day someone moved. Every day someone longed for more family time. Every day someone left a job incomplete. Every day someone grieved. However, I knew that everyday stress didn't give ulcers to everybody. My stomach weakness indicated I wasn't doing too well at living with everyday stress.

Had I courted stress as a strange but sacred companion that drove me to bump into and leap over my limits? Was it my motivation to always be stressed? Was I manipulated by the seductive power of the stressors? However I answered these questions, my stress swelled to the heated intensity of a volcano bursting into expression, unconcerned about its fallout. I, like an active volcano, was ready to rid myself of the lava of stress. I was willing to face the void the ejected stress would leave.

No Longer a Prisoner to Stress

The cold snowy spring night was good reason to be sweatered and cozy by an open fire. I watched the embers and flames in restful familiarity. Medicine had relieved my stomach pain. My journey to revisit my stress had exhausted me; yet, at the same time, it had calmed me. I felt that I could survive and live again with the pleasure of being a fully functioning person. I was feeling more free. In the freed-up and relaxed moment, an experience at Spandau Prison with Rudolph Hess sprang from my subconscience.

Spandau Prison was everything but freedom. It was a massive, high-security prison built to house six hundred prisoners in West Berlin, Germany. Its high walls were capped with guard towers, all tied together with barbed wire. It was built so no one could ever escape.

Rudolph Hess was the sole prisoner at Spandau Prison. He

would never be free. As the intimate friend, officer, and right-hand man of Adolf Hitler, Hess was probably the most renowned prisoner in the world.

In 1971, as officer of the guard at Spandau Prison, I had the duty of walking with Mr. Hess twice a day. We walked together in the prison garden. I entered the garden through two ten-foot-high iron doors, shut and locked them, and then accompanied Mr. Hess for thirty minutes under the constant protective eyes of the Berlin Brigade guards.

I remember that as the gates shut, the loud clanging sounds of closure echoed throughout the prison garden and yards. As I turned the large key, I always felt locked in, somewhat like a prisoner myself. As we walked, I would reach into my pocket and feel the keys just to assure myself that I could get out when I chose to do so.

Mr. Hess stayed for the rest of his life locked in Spandau Prison, locked in because of poor choices he had made in his life. He could not set himself free. Yet I had the keys to set myself free.

The everyday stress in my life had been left unattended to such a degree that it had become my prison. I had the keys to get out at Spandau Prison. Remembering that, I now asked myself if I had the keys to set myself free from my prison of stress.

That night, I concluded that I did. The keys to relieve my stress were the elements of everyday faith. The keys of everyday faith would become essential in my return to resilience in the face of everyday stress.

4
Unlocking the Prison Gates

Four weeks later, X rays proved my ulcer was gone. I was relieved that the pain had subsided, and now the relief of "the cure" made me believe positive things could again happen to me. I could now get back to living, not just recuperating.

In comparison to other stress effects, my stress damage had been minor. I lost only one and one-half workdays. I missed no preaching events. I still had a family, job, home, and community. In comparison, my stress had cost me little. On the other hand, my stress and its effects upon me were substantial.

I can remember a vivid scene in the movie *E.T.* Sitting on the bicycle handlebars as Elliot pedaled himself and E.T. out of the pursuing police officers' reach, E.T. questioned whether they were in danger. Wanting to make sure E.T. understood their dilemma, Elliot responded: "This is *for real!*"

My stress and its effect were not make-believe. They were *for real.* The pain and fear resulting from the ulcer proved vivid reminders that I wanted to get on top of the stress.

I was not so naive as to think that everything was OK or that I was back to a balanced life. I felt nervous. I feared I might be overwhelmed, lose control, and become stressed out again to the point of ulcer recurrence or something worse. I knew I had to practice everyday faith as I lived in, for, and toward God. The very thought of relieving stress brought more stress! Would my faith be sufficient? I had more than enough everyday stress to challenge faith. Did I have the faith necessary to live abundantly in the face of everyday stress?

In his classic *Christ and Culture*, Reinhold Niebuhr formulated several possibilities in the relationship of Christ and culture in the life of the Christian. Christ and culture could form a balanced influence for a Christian. Culture could dominate Christ in influence on a Christian, or Christ could bear more influence than culture over the life of a Christian.

At this hour in my life, everyday stress and everyday faith competed for influence. If I allowed everyday stress to dominate everyday faith, that would be self-defeating and destructive. I had had enough of that. I could allow everyday stress and everyday faith to have equal influence on me. That would appear neutral, but it would really be destructive. Or I could choose to allow everyday faith to become more dominant than everyday stress.

I decided on Christ over culture. Everyday faith over everyday stress.

Now, to live out the decision. How would I allow what I believed to make a difference in my behavior? How would I take God-breathed life and live it in the pace and pulse of God?

I Took Time for Myself

During the process of anticipating death, I began to appreciate time as a real gift. Professionally, time had most often been my enemy. It reminded me of limits and teased me by keeping my "incomplete" list longer than my "jobs done" list. I knew stress release took time and called for a wise use of time.

Learning to take time for myself was not easy, but I needed to relieve my ordinarily stressed time. I needed time to do nothing or to do whatever I wanted. I discovered that a minute vacation could be rich experience, a time capsule full of eternity. The simple act of taking time taught me how much time I really had. I had been handcuffed by the self-defeating stress of poor time management whenever I said, "I don't have time."

Taking time to rest was a first step on my journey. My body demanded it. At last my mind gave in, and I began to rest. Adequate sleep relaxed face muscles and let me smile again. Rest delighted my body with new bursts of energy long ago forgotten by an exhausted, overly stressed soul. Rest became a matter of faith. It took faith for me to stop and rest. It took faith to believe God could get along without my frantic efforts! How arrogant and inconsistent with Christ I had become to think I should work all the time. Rest became for me a long, slow, and overdue confession.

Taking time for myself, even in rest, even as confession, proved difficult. I had to make myself take time for myself. The urge "to do" and to be busy kept creeping back up on me. So I had to schedule rest time, and often I had to fill that time with relaxation activities.

Bicycling

I began to bicycle.

During the eight months following recovery from my ulcer, I bicycled some two thousand miles. Quite a journey of stress relief!

I bicycled because I couldn't make myself just sit and rest. I needed something to do. I also needed to get away from the telephone and to be totally unavailable for brief times. Personal challenge, play, exercise, new scenery, time alone—bicycling offered me all of that.

I rode mile after mile in the Blue Ridge Mountains of Western North Carolina until my leg muscles began to feel like muscles again. I smelled trees and grass and plants I had never before noticed. Bicycling was good for me. It offered a shock absorber to my stress.

Prayer: A Stream of Silence Amidst the Noise

Back in the office, however, I could feel the weight of visits to make, calls to return, sermons to prepare, committee work to follow up on, community events to attend. On some days, five minutes in the office made me feel I needed five hours on the bicycle just to maintain resilience.

Prayer has most often been my reaction to the weight of work and office demands. It is the hinge upon which everyday faith swings. For me, prayer is the stream of silence in the noise. I must have reduced my praying to dangerously low levels for stress to get so out of proportion.

Prayer proved another first step in my everyday faith. It allowed light in the darkness, direction in the confusion, and stillness in the stress. It was the first and the last act of the day. It happened all during the day.

I had never before needed a schedule for prayer, as I had always had a sense of God's presence at any time, and that sense served as prayer for me. But because my life had so gotten out of sync, I scheduled at least three prayer times a day.

When I did not want to pray, I prayed for the desire to pray. Often I prayed for the will to will His will. At other times I prayed that I could simply wait upon the One who waited for me.

In my stress-relief journey, prayer became a stream of silence amidst all the noise, a stream of silence in which much was said, heard, felt, and experienced.

Making Worship Count

Perhaps I had made an idol out of stress. It felt good being overbooked. Perhaps it made me feel important to be seen as a pastor who gave so much. I was worshiping stress and wanting people to worship me—or at least, to love me. In retrospect, I see that I had functioned as if I didn't need God. Much rest and tough prayer enabled me to see this.

To regain proper perspective in worship, I had to see God as Creator and myself as creature. I had to remember His unlimitedness and my limitedness. I had to allow Him to love me, ulcer and all. I had to trust that He could and would heal me, love me, and accept me after such a stupid and unfaithful time in my life.

As a worship leader, I became more conscious of needing the public faith announcement. I was strengthened as I listened to and joined with the congregation in hymn singing, Scripture reading, and prayer. I allowed that spoken-out-loud faith to focus on my weaknesses. I was being renewed in the very worship events I led.

Public worship served as punctuation marks for daily periods of private worship. During the early weeks of major stress relief, my private worship taught me much. I was overstressed because I had lost the significance of praise. I had become too busy to praise God. Praising took time, time away from things I was convinced were more important. I had taken God for granted. I had just assumed His gifts would continue. I had had no time for praise, thanksgiving, confession, repentance, contemplation, or commitment. I had lived several months of my life with little worship. It was like life without an energy source, life without direction, life without communion.

The most helpful worship exercises in the early stages of stress relief were constant presence, confessing my sins of inattention to Him, allowing His word to come to me in silence and stillness, and receiving those words as assurance and guidance for my day. Praise, thanksgiving, and commitment proved the result of that worship. Celebration of Christ became more constant. In this type of worship-communion, no stress seemed overwhelming. I was, again, drinking from the Water of life. And my thirst was being quenched.

Regaining the Discipline of Study

Prayer and worship lead to more study. With a restlessness in prayer and worship, study had been almost impossible. In order to study the faith, I had to have an open channel to the Author of my faith. I had to love God with all my mind, as well as study His Word and the history of the church's response to His Word. I knew that if I didn't use my mind to study, it would again be filled and cluttered with stressors begging for more attention than they deserved. Faith had to be on the cutting edge of where I lived life. A dusty, closed-Bible approach to life was no good. For me to be on the cutting edge, faith had to swell from the core of my being. Study enabled this to be true for me.

Reformer Martin Luther believed the Word brought reform. The same proved true in my journey. I believe the Word feeds the mind with facts, defines the belief, announces the value, and persuades behavior. Reform and (as in my case) stress relief developed through the same process.

Ministry Perspective Regained

The stress relief through ministry came most clearly as I re-believed that in loving God, we feel a call to love people. To love people, I knew I must exert energy on their behalf and well-being. As I exerted energy to minister to others through praying, counseling, visiting, serving, and leading, I came to a new appreciation of the grace and love of God that flowed through me to them. Not only did that grace and love minister to others; it also ministered, in the form of a profound healing, to me. Ministry is the doing of the faith. It is clear evidence that belief influences behavior.

Relationship: Taking It Easy on Myself

Ministry cannot be done in a vacuum. It is done person to person.

Relationship has a sense of the sacred in it. It's a very sacred thing for me to know another person, to see the image of God in that person, to be known by another person, and to have that person see God's image in me. Relationship is a sacred encounter in which two discuss significant and insignificant values.

Relationship is God's gift of grace for us when we feel lonely and alone. Several relationship gifts have come my way: a caring congregation who is patient and kind; a ministers' support group who is probing and supportive; close friends who give time for mutual delight; community board members who have stayed together through tough times, carving relationship in the most unlikely assortment of people; an encouraging family; and reunion with friends and former church parishioners.

In stress relief, it is not so important that I be able to *define* relationship. It has been essential, however, that I *experience* it. Relationship, more than anything else, makes me take it easy on myself.

Clarifying God's Call: Am I Where He Wants Me?

Was I where God wanted me to be? Was I doing what He wanted me to do? I could have no constant stress relief without knowing this.

How could I be sure it was God who said: "Come to Boone, Steven, and let Me bless you." Quite honestly, even if God had called me, I didn't care for the "blessing" of excessive stress and an ulcer!

I knew well the stages in the call process: God speaks, I listen, I clarify, I make a decision, I act out the decision, and I receive the grace of God in the obedient response.

Over and over again it all seemed to check out. I felt God's leading me to Boone. I believed I had listened to Him. I clarified what He had called me to do: to go to a special congregation of great gift whose members were momentarily wounded with grief; to use my gifts of listening, perception, proclamation, and leadership to serve them. I had decided to do as I felt led.

In the meantime, I had become so overwhelmed with stress that I lost the clear focus and certainty of specific call. Attention to everyday faith enabled me to believe, once again, that I was where God had led me.

Forgiveness

The last chapter in my journey of stress relief was forgiveness. I believe Christ's forgiveness is threefold.

First, God has forgiven me for all the selfish moves and wrong choices that led me into the episode of stress overload. His forgiveness served as an invitation to, again, be His fully functioning person.

Secondly, I had to forgive people who abused me, assumed upon me, took me for granted, and neglected me. And I had to ask people to forgive me when I treated them the same way. I knew that failure to forgive led to resentment, and resentment was heavy stress that I did not need.

Thirdly, I had to forgive myself. I had to live as a "forgiven one." Since God forgave me, I could easily forgive others and receive their forgiveness. But to forgive myself was more difficult. It did not come immediately. I had hated the mistake of stress overload and the resulting ulcer. I didn't like myself for either factor. But the rhythm of prayer, worship, ministry, relationship, and call clarification kept leading to one last stanza: Forgive yourself and celebrate your life in Christ.

And somewhere in the midst of prayer, it came. "OK, I'm forgiven!" Over and over I said it! Everyday faith was having its effect.

Everyday faith was enriching, blessing, enabling, and reassuring me. Everyday faith had become a great influence over everyday stress, not merely dissolving it but countering it. Faith reacted to it and enabled me to be faithful in the midst of it. I knew my world would continue to be stressful, and Christ could continue to make me faithful. This everyday faith was no one-time fix or a single episode of heavy-duty religion. Its strength lay in the everyday faithfulness of God the Father to me. It necessitated an everyday awareness on my part. Its journey has often led me to ask: "Who am I?" And though the immediate answers to that question often change, my journey into everyday faith has led me, at this junction, to answer in this way:

Who Am I?

I am one running into stress
      from stress
      with stress.
I am stillness through which
  His life storms move.
I am storm
  His stillness settles.
Who am I?
  I am child of His image.
  I am glad recipient of grace.
  I am created as gift of grace.
Who am I?
  I am called one
    coming to terms with my gifts
      confessing my needs.
Who am I?
  I am a voice
    through which He speaks.
  I am millions of words read,
    thousands of words remembered,
    hundreds of words loved,
    a few words given.
  I am muteness molded into a
    river of Something that
      has to be said.
Who am I?
  I am perception
    immediate and gentle.
  I am reed through which
      His Spirit
    breathes and flows and blows.

Who am I?
  I am seeker of His will.
  I am journey
     toward and in
        obedient faith.
  I am thankful, for grace.
Who am I?
  I am but a moment of time
     sensitive to all of His time.
  I am not alone.
     I am person being met.
  I am given.
     I am received.
  I receive.
     I give.
Who am I?
  I am given to oceans of people
     and always drawn to the beach of solitude.
  I am occasionally extrovert
     and thoroughly introvert.
  I am teacher longing to be taught.
Who am I?
  I am human man dealing with priesthood.
  I am priest dealing with humanness.
  I am His called one
     His rebellious one
     His questioning one,
        But always,
I am His.

We now turn this book out to you. We have told you our stories of stress and our journeys of faith. Up to this point, we have spoken with two voices. We reach out to you now with one voice.

Perhaps you, too, are hurting. Perhaps the burden of undue and everyday stress has become your constant companion, and you need and want to find rest from it.

We believe you *can* overcome much of your everyday stress. This is the reason for this book. We are finding the answer for everyday stress relief through a developing everyday faith. It is working for us. We trust it will also work for you.

We hope the remainder of this book will inspire you, guide you, and give you some solid and practical suggestions for relieving much of your everyday stress and for building your everyday faith.

That is our prayer.

Section III
Everyday Stress, Everyday Faith

We look not to the things that are seen
but to the things that are unseen;
for the things that are seen are transient,
but the things that are unseen are eternal.

2 Corinthians 4:18

5
What Is Everyday Stress?

"It . . . seems as if our society were designed to break the human spirit," wrote Arthur Gish in his book *Beyond the Rat Race.* "Rather than a *style of life,* it might be called a *style of death*" (italics mine).[1]

Everyday stress. You certainly don't need us to tell you what everyday stress is! If you're human, you already know a lot about everyday stress. For everyday stress is a part of living in this fast-paced, technological, fast-food society.

L. E. Hinkle defined stress as force, strain, and strong effort placed upon a person.[2]

We know about force, strain, and strong effort. They are the daily demands and expectations that are laid upon us by others, that we lay upon ourselves, and that we lay upon other people.

Good Stress, Bad Stress

We tend to think of stress as always bad for us. Stress, however, can be good or bad. If you've just bought a new car or accepted a new job, if you have been just married or birthed a longed-for child, then you've experienced good stress. Hans Selye called this good stress "eustress."[3]

Think of eustress as the glow of ambition, creativity, desire, or excitement that gets you up out of bed in the morning. Good stress "is like heat in your body or in the engine of your automobile. Some of it is vitally necessary to the proper function of your body or your car."[4]

According to Selye, "distress," however, is the negative side of stress. Distress is the scratch on your new car, the cigar-smoking, too-demanding boss at your new job, the first argument with your new bride, and the longed-for newborn who sleeps all day and cries all night. Think of distress as the lack of ambition, creativity, desire, or excitement that keeps you *between* the bed covers in the morning and makes you late for work. Too much distress can cause you big problems.

We enjoy eustress. This good stress proves no problem for us. We don't enjoy distress, however, and we often don't know what to do about it. So let's talk about the problem of distress.

The Enemy Distress

Thomas Holmes and Minoru Masuda have done extensive work in the study of distress. They've put together a simple stress-rating scale, listing some forty-three major causes of stress. Let us give you their top ten most devastating stressors: the death of a spouse, divorce, marital separation, a jail term, the death of a close family member, personal injury or illness, marriage, being fired at work, marital reconciliation, and retirement.[5]

On the other hand, stress seminar participants tell us their leading everyday stressors are confrontation, deadlines, too much to do, making decisions, making a mistake, speaking before a group, and saying no.[6]

Just what is everyday stress? It is the pressure, tension, misgivings, fear, nervousness, dread, hardships, anxieties, and general restlessness of the everyday. This everyday undue stress can cause health problems that range from

tension headaches to low back pains, or, as one expert ob-
served: "a tension headache that has slipped down the
back!"

While *major* stressors can literally knock us off our feet, the
minor irritations of everyday life can be even more hazardous
to our health. "Most researchers today accept that major
stressful events do indeed take a toll on health. But the latest
research suggests that the average person is as likely to be
'nibbled to death' by everyday hassles as overwhelmed by
tragedies."[7]

Everyday stress begins at birth, as we endure the hardship
of the birth itself, and continues throughout our lifetime.
Everyday stress is so everyday that we often fail to see it.
Indeed, what we don't know, what we can't see, *can,* in fact,
hurt us!

What Is Your Particular Stress?

You may or may not agree with Holmes and Masuda and
the stress seminar participants. No doubt, you could write
your own stress-rating scale! Someone once described stress
this way: "I feel like a bullfrog sitting on the freeway during
the 5:00 PM traffic rush with my 'hopper' broken"!

That's probably the best definition of distress yet! Have
you ever felt like that?

Just what is *your* particular stress right now?

As a mother at home with preschoolers all day, you might
say stress is: "Wet diapers hanging from wet bottoms, oat-
meal splattered all over the table, too much to do, and not
enough energy to get it all done." (Erma Bombeck once
summed up motherhood in one word: *exhaustion!* You might
agree!)

As a parent of teenagers, you might say something quite
different. Stress is "worrying about my son driving and stay-

ing out too late." Stress is the "fear of alcohol, drugs, negative peer pressure, grades, premature sex, and the risk of disease."

If you work outside the home in an unfulfilling job, you might describe stress as sheer boredom: the "blue-collar blues," the "white-collar woes." You may daily experience the uncreative, "dulling effect of the assembly line, . . . the watchful eyes of the foreman." Boredom can distress you wherever you work: home, office, factory, restaurant, in any job.

Studs Terkel wrote that "most people are unhappy at their work. They have chosen it in order . . . to make a living far more than to express themselves."[8] The daily stifling of the creative expression that yearns to surface in you can cause much frustration and everyday stress.

Everyday stress abounds! It can be caused by traffic jams, poor health, worry about the future, grief, anticipating divorce, intruding in-laws, loud neighbors, envy, sadness, chemical dependency, making decisions, homesickness, loneliness, a promiscuous spouse, rebellious children, unresolved anger, a move from home, guilt, lack of self-esteem, feeling distant from God, or just a bad night's sleep.

We can experience everyday stress when we watch the evening news. Our world's violent and uncivilized day-to-day conflicts can cause us to feel sad, angry, helpless, and frustrated.

Everyday stress. We're all on the same freeway here: bullfrogs with our "hoppers" broken. Eugene Kennedy said it well in his book *The Trouble with Being Human:* "The first principle in being human . . . is based on the universal and exceptionless truth that *nobody has it all together.* It only looks that way" (italics mine).[9]

Perhaps we could put everyday stress into four main categories: personal, spiritual, financial, and relational.

Personal Stress

We feel stress in the everyday process of growing up. With every life stage, every life-changing event, every passage of rite or time, we experience a different form of stress. Can you remember the stress you felt when you marched off to the first day of the first grade? Or the butterflies you met on your first date, first job, or wedding day? What about the first time you drove a car alone? We find stress not only in our life's "firsts" but in the everydayness of the everyday, simply because we are daily growing and changing and experiencing life anew.

Personal stress may be caused by having to come to terms with limits. Much of our society has assumed a "life-in-the-fast-lane" life-style. Many Americans seem to want to live as Europeans drive on the autobahns—fast, free, and with no speed limits. Yet we are created with limits. We are limited by time itself, for each of our days contains only twenty-four hours. We are limited physically, for our bodies demand regular sleep, rest, care, and a decent diet. And as Christians, we are limited in our personal wants and desires. We can't simply "do what feels good when it feels good." For we are in Christ, and Christ is in us. And that oneship with Him limits us morally. Anytime we allow ourselves to push or exceed those limits, we can expect personal stress.

Everyday personal stress also results when life's most basic human needs are not fulfilled.

Abraham Maslow categorized these basic human needs as physiological, safety, love, self-esteem, and self-actualization.[10]

Our physiological needs are life-sustaining needs: air,

food, water, and life-supporting temperatures. These essentials give us life, human energy. Without them we wouldn't survive.

Only after we satisfy our physiological needs can we begin to concentrate on fulfilling our needs for safety. At this level, safety and protection are principal concerns. We need security, stability, dependency, and protection. We also need structure, order, law, and limits to protect us from the surrounding everyday chaos, fear, and anxiety of life.

After the needs of human survival and safety are met, we can move on to our love needs. As humans, we yearn for contact and touch and intimacy and family and home and roots and neighbors and friends. We want to belong to somebody. "It is not good that the man should be alone," Genesis 2:18 declares. The failure to satisfy our love and belonging needs often results in pathology, which is, simply put, the illness of the deficiency of love.

After our love needs are met, we're ready to move on to higher needs, the needs of self-regard and self-esteem. It's the "something" in us that yearns for respect, reputation, and prestige. We want to feel competent, strong, and independent. How a person meets this need determines how capable, adequate, and self-confident he or she feels.

Lastly, we reach the "being" needs, as Maslow termed them. We begin to move toward self-actualization. These are the needs for "truth, goodness, beauty, wholeness, dichotomy-transcendence, aliveness, uniqueness, perfection, simplicity, richness, effortlessness, playfulness, and self-sufficiency."[11] We want to experience "peak" moments, the happy and wonderful and mystical moments of life when we are freed up to be more creative, spontaneous, and expressive.[12]

Spiritual Stress

Just as we look in the mirror each morning and form some self-esteem evaluation about our personal selves, we may also daily size up ourselves spiritually. We strive to become Christlike, yet how hard it can be for us! The "mirror, mirror on the wall" shows us what we most like and dislike about our person. Our spiritual mirror, God's mirror, reflects our spiritual likes and dislikes about ourselves. It's not fun to look at our physical or spiritual warts and blemishes. And often we can't quickly or easily change the parts we dislike. This takes time and work. So we must live with them as we work to change them, and that can be quite stressful.

Another great spiritual stressor is loneliness.

"At the most basic level of our existence we are all strangers crying out for recognition, for acceptance, reaching out eagerly for signs of friendship and hospitality," wrote Harold Warlick in his book *Conquering Loneliness.*[13]

Loneliness is estrangement from God and from one another. We can experience a lonely emptiness, and this emptiness, for many, proves an everyday stress that announces itself with sharp-edged jabs to the soul longing for intimacy.

We often struggle to know how to pray and to understand this faith we try to live. "If only God had strong, loving flesh-and-blood arms that He could wrap around us," a lonely woman once told a friend. "He does," her friend responded. "We can feel His arms through the strong, loving arms of a friend."

Loneliness causes spiritual stress. Lack of time with God, for God, also produces spiritual stress. When we decide to live our lives for God, we learn that spiritual devotion takes time. Scheduled quiet time to pray, contemplate, meditate, study, and worship does not fit well into our nation of people "on the run." We are a people who describe "patience" as "waiting in a hurry."[14] Building a close relationship with God cannot be done in a hurry. It demands everyday *hours,* not mere minutes.

And, sadly, a less-than-close relationship with God can throw all of life out of sync. When that happens, we can be tossed about by an ocean of distressful waves without the benefit of a sturdy life Preserver.

Financial Stress

Financial stress results from underpaid employment or lack of employment, an absence of money-managing skills, an overspending spouse or self, a striving to "keep up with the Joneses," living beyond financial means, high medical or emergency costs, inadequate retirement funds, and many other circumstances in which cash is short.

Much stress results from money itself.

"Money . . . is one of the most unsatisfying of possessions. It takes away some cares, no doubt; but it brings with it quite as many cares as it takes away. There is the trouble in the getting of it. There is anxiety in the keeping of it. There are temptations in the use of it. There is guilt in the abuse of it. There is sorrow in the losing of it. There is perplexity in the disposing of it," wrote J. C. Ryle.[15]

If you are presently under financial stress, know that you aren't alone. Almost half of Americans today are suffering from the frustrating stress caused by financial debt. *Money Magazine* reported that "almost 44 percent of families are concerned that they might owe more than they should."[16]

The Stresses of Relationship

As soon as you enter into it, relationship spells S-T-R-E-S-S. We notice at a young age that people around us have opinions, desires, needs, and quirks that are different from ours and that they often come into direct competition with ours. In relationship, we learn quickly we must consider someone else besides ourselves.

Perhaps the greatest relational stress these days is found within the family. Consider the stress caused by single parenting, deciding roles in marriage, parenting and disciplining children, living and teaching moral values, trying to communicate, nursing a sick or handicapped family member, or relating to and caring for in-laws. The potential for family-related stress seems endless.

The American Institute of Stress recognized: "Every day, the world bombards us with stress. That's why your home should be a haven, a place to balance yourself out and recharge your batteries. But that won't happen if your home life also happens to be stressful."[17]

Often, home, marriage, and family don't offer us a haven of rest from stress. We can look at the current divorce rates and know that things are not fully alive and well in the state of family affairs. Every day couples cope with threats of divorce and miserable marriages—marriages far removed from "wedding-day dreams." "Living happily ever after is, for them, something that happens only in fairy tales. For many, marriage [seems] all too formidable a task."[18]

Everyday family stress can begin before you even get out of bed in the morning. One spouse might be up making noise while the other spouse tries to sleep. Family stress continues at the breakfast table when each member wants a different brand of cereal and a different fat content of milk. Good moods, bad moods, dressing children for school, rushing to make lunches and find homework, early morning traffic. By the end of the day, after racing from after-school ball games to swimming practice to Cub Scouts, a family might easily spell relief R-O-L-A-I-D-S.

Consider the stress of the two-paycheck family. The Department of Labor statistics show that "62 percent of women with children under age 18 are employed."[19] Each parent is "professional," given to and often consumed by the job. Too often, it seems, we *live* at work, and we *visit* home.

The stress load on the working mother alone is titanic. "Among . . . working mothers, tales abound of guilt; of the inability to juggle the demands of work, children, a husband and a home without being fatigued and feeling inadequate."[20] And who can measure the effects all of this is having on the husband?

The guilt, fatigue, and overwork generated by two hardworking parents can drastically reduce the time available for knowing each other in the family. Intimacy in marriage and family can be stunted. We may grasp for a moment or two of "quality time," having long ago given up on any kind of future "quantity time."

* * *

What is your particular stress right now? Does it fall most heavily into the category of personal, spiritual, financial, relational, or just general stress?

We have compiled a simple everyday stress test that may help you to determine in what areas of your life you feel most stressed. We invite you to take the test before you begin the next chapter.

Notes

1. Arthur G. Gish, *Beyond the Rat Race* (Scottsdale, Pa.: Herald Press, 1973), p. 20.

2. L. E. Hinkle, "The Concept of Stress in the Biological and Social Sciences," *Science, Medicine & Man,* Vol. I, 1973, pp. 31-48.

3. As quoted by Wayne E. Oates, *Managing Your Stress* (Indianapolis, Ind.: Bierce Associates, Inc., 1983), p. 3.

4. Ibid.

5. Ibid., p. 29.

6. Steven C. Carreker. (Information gleaned from stress seminars, 1984, 1985, 1986.)

7. Norma Peterson, "Daily Hassles Are Hazardous," *Reader's Digest,* Apr. 1987, p. 76.

8. As quoted by Eugene Kennedy, *The Trouble with Being Human* (Garden City, N.Y.: Image Books, 1986), p. 134.

9. Ibid., p. 35.

10. As quoted by Abraham Maslow, *Toward a Psychology of Being* (New York: Nostrand, 1968), pp. 21-125.

11. As quoted by Abraham Maslow, *Religions, Values, and Peak Experiences* (New York: Viking Press, 1970), pp. 91-96.

12. As quoted by Steven Camp Carreker, *Discipling in Relationship to Maslow's Hierarchy of Needs,* unpublished Ministry Research Project, Dec. 1981, pp. 15-21.

13. Harold C. Warlick, Jr., *Conquering Loneliness* (Waco: Word Books, 1979), p. 15.

14. Dr. Wayne E. Oates. (Quote gleaned from class lectures, Spring 1984.)

15. Denise George, *The Christian as a Consumer* (Philadelphia: The Westminister Press, 1984), p. 26.

16. "When You're Too Far in Debt," *Reader's Digest,* Sept. 1987, p. 50.

17. "39 Ways to De-stress Your Home Life," *Prevention Magazine,* The American Institute of Stress, Vol. 39, No. 9, Sept. 1987, p. 34.

18. Diana S. Richmond Garland and David E. Garland, *Beyond Companionship, Christians in Marriage* (Philadelphia: The Westminister Press, 1986), p. 7.

19. Betty Cuniberti, "Are Working Mothers Really Pioneers?" *The Courier-Journal,* 16 Aug. 1987, p. H6.

20. Ibid.

My Everyday Stress Test
Mark the following questions with "true" or "false."

General Stress Areas	True	False
1. I spend too much time doing things that don't interest me.	___	___
2. I'm probably depressed but don't want to admit it.	___	___
3. I'm often exhausted.	___	___
4. I'm unhappy a lot lately.	___	___
5. Tension is common for me.	___	___
6. I eat too much.	___	___
7. Often I feel angry.	___	___
8. I worry a lot.	___	___
9. I'm often restless.	___	___
10. I've contemplated suicide.	___	___
11. Often I feel afraid.	___	___
12. I criticize very quickly.	___	___
13. I feel guilty.	___	___
14. I dread getting up.	___	___
15. My life goals aren't focused.	___	___

Personal Stress		
1. It is not easy for me to say no.	___	___
2. I frequently feel lonely.	___	___
3. I never seem to have enough hours in the day.	___	___
4. I really don't like myself today.	___	___
5. I don't have enough time for myself.	___	___

Spiritual Stress		
1. My prayers make little difference.	___	___
2. I feel spiritually bankrupt.	___	___
3. I don't know how to make my faith count.	___	___
4. I simply cannot apply Scripture to everyday life.	___	___
5. My church life brings little relief to my everyday stress.	___	___

Stress in Relationships		
1. My spouse and I are too distant.	___	___
2. My neighborhood is cold.	___	___
3. My family doesn't really know me.	___	___
4. I never have enough time with people.	___	___
5. I don't know my family as well as I would like.	___	___

Job-Related Stress

1. I don't enjoy the work I do. ____ ____
2. I'm not paid fairly. ____ ____
3. I'm not excited about my job. ____ ____
4. I don't get along with my boss these days. ____ ____
5. My work isn't very important to the world. ____ ____

Financial Stress

1. I don't have a disciplined savings habit. ____ ____
2. I'm financially strapped. ____ ____
3. I feel uneasy about my retirement. ____ ____
4. I never seem to have enough money. ____ ____
5. I'm always spending more money than I
   should. ____ ____

To interpret your everyday stress test, look at the number of times you answered with a "true." Each "true" answer is the result of stress.

In the "General Stress Areas," each "true" answer gives you an indicator of your general everyday stress level.

How did you answer in the specific categories: personal, spiritual, relationship, job, and financial? Again, each "true" answer indicates stress. The categories will help you determine in which area of life you are presently most stressful.

6
What Everyday Stress
Can Do to You

Everyday stress. Here are the facts:

Stress is being "increasingly linked to the development and course of cancer, high blood pressure, heart attacks, diabetes, asthma, allergies, ulcers, colitis, alcoholism, smoking, obesity, headaches, backaches and many other diseases."[1]

Most of us are presently suffering the effects of everyday stress. One study showed that "from 75 to 90 percent of all visits to primary-care physicians are for stress-related disorders."[2]

Too much stress will make you ill. If you are operating on stress overload, you can expect to become sick. Irritating daily hassles can wear you down like a car engine racing at full throttle with the emergency brake on. You can expect to become just as ill with these repeated, daily aggravations as you would from major, life-changing traumas.[3]

Beware: The Symptoms of Everyday Stress

Whether stress is personal, spiritual, financial, or relational, we most often see the enemy distress after it hits. Our body responds to our rat race life-styles by means of physical symptoms. Everyday stress ignored produces a variety of destructive maladies. For instance, if you are under terrific, uninterrupted stress, you'll probably age more quickly, be sick more often, and experience some changes in your sexual

73

behavior. You won't be as happy about life or as efficient in your job, and you'll slowly begin to withdraw from people. You may find yourself arguing more with family and friends, criticizing them unjustly. You will probably feel sad and tired and not be able to adequately explain it.

Take a moment and listen to your body if you are experiencing these symptoms. It is struggling to tell you to stop and take a personal inventory. Your stress load is getting too high.

Depression

If you don't stop and listen, however, everyday stress can swell into normal depression. Normal depression is, in contrast to clinical depression, generally low-grade. (Clinical depression goes deeper into despair and signals a disorder more than does normal depression. A clinically depressed person needs medical help.) Normal depression comes and goes and usually leaves no permanent trace. However, whenever it comes and lingers, normal depression is no welcomed guest.

Andrew Lester considered depression a "crisis" and wrote: "Depression robs life of happiness, excitement, and joy. . . . We get moody, refuse to talk, withdraw from those we love, [and] dislike ourselves."[4]

The depressed person screams on the inside for expression and for the benefit of being heard. Hopelessness, however, generally silences the screams. Paranoia, feelings of inadequacy, even death thoughts plague the mind. The depressed person gives expression to his futility through sleeplessness, stomach pains, compulsive overeating or not eating, overwork or underwork, and a significant loss of normal human emotion.

As a victim of depression, you will become increasingly

unhappy. You may build strong brick walls around yourself, so you can't reach out to others, and they can't reach in to you. No doubt, you will feel spiritually bored and empty, too. You may wonder where God is, and if your life holds any meaning at all.

Burnout

When not controlled, everyday stress can grow beyond depression into a more dreadful emotional stage: burnout.

Burned out, we lose our ambition, enthusiasm, creativity, and commitment. We become calloused with a cynical, critical attitude. We feel we are no longer effective anywhere. We lose the capacity to be good evaluators of our effectiveness. We dread going to work; we dread coming home from work. We suffer from intense exhaustion. We feel God is nowhere near us. We cry out for a lack of purpose in life, some reason for our existence. We lose inner control of ourselves and feel angry and guilty about the loss. Thoughts of suicide, only contemplated in depression, are now seriously considered.

Victims of burnout can probably no longer correct the problem themselves. At this point, they will need help.

The picture painted by everyday stress isn't a pretty one. It's a portrait of despair, despondency, sorrow, and unhappiness—of gloominess, dejection, melancholy, and misery. The overstressed person will know discouragement, hopelessness, and desperation.

Where Is Our Hope, Then?

These are the distressing facts about too much daily stress in your life. Perhaps just reading this chapter on "everyday stress" has caused you more everyday stress! We hope not. The magnitude of distress we can encounter, however, is frightening and discouraging, isn't it? While we can't control all the stress that hits us from every side, we can choose to control at least some of it. We can also learn to control much of our response to stress. What can you do about the every-day hassles of stress that you can control?

We believe you can set yourself free from many of the pressures of everyday stress by means of an active everyday faith. Our hope lies in the person of Jesus Christ.

You need no longer be locked in your cell of everyday stress. For, at this very moment, you can hold the keys to your own Spandau Prison. You, too, can set yourself free from much of the stress that imprisons you.

We pray you will journey with us through yet another chapter, the chapter that leads to Hope.

* * *

To help you determine the amount of stress you are presently undergoing, we have included the well-known Holmes/Masuda "Social Readjustment Rating Scale."[5]

Holmes and Masuda have given a certain number of "points" to each of their forty-three stressful events. They have concluded that if, at any given time, your total adds up to 300 points or beyond, you are in the stress danger zone and at risk of becoming sick.

Please take a few minutes to read their rating scale, circle your present stresses, and then add up your total points.

Social Readjustment Rating Scale

Rank	Life Event	Mean Value
1.	Death of spouse	100
2.	Divorce	73
3.	Marital Separation	65
4.	Jail Term	63
5.	Death of Close Family Member	63
6.	Personal Injury or Illness	53
7.	Marriage	50
8.	Fired at Work	47
9.	Marital Reconciliation	45
10.	Retirement	45
11.	Change in Health of Family Member	44
12.	Pregnancy	40
13.	Sex Difficulties	39
14.	Gain of New Family Member	39
15.	Business Readjustment	39
16.	Change in Financial State	38
17.	Death of Close Friend	37
18.	Change to Different Line of Work	36
19.	Change in Number of Arguments with Spouse	35
20.	Mortgage over $10,000	31
21.	Foreclosure of Mortgage or Loan	30
22.	Change in Responsibilities at Work	29
23.	Son or Daughter Leaving Home	29
24.	Trouble with In-Laws	29
25.	Outstanding Personal Achievement	28
26.	Spouse Begins or Stops Work	26
27.	Begin or End School	26
28.	Change in Living Conditions	25
29.	Revision of Personal Habits	24
30.	Trouble with Boss	23
31.	Change in Work Hours or Conditions	20
32.	Change in Residence	20
33.	Change in Schools	20
34.	Change in Recreation	19
35.	Change in Church Activities	19
36.	Change in Social Activities	18
37.	Mortgage or Loan Less Than $10,000	17
38.	Change in Sleeping Habits	16
39.	Change in Number of Family Get-Togethers	15
40.	Change in Eating Habits	15
41.	Vacation	13
42.	Christmas	12
43.	Minor Violations of the Law	11

Notes

1. Susan Zarrow, "Stress: The Facts," *Prevention Magazine,* Vol. 39, No. 9, Sept. 1987, p. 86.

2. Ibid.

3. Ibid.

4. Andrew D. Lester, *It Hurts So Bad, Lord!* (Nashville: Broadman Press, 1976), p. 9.

5. Wayne E. Oates, *Managing Your Stress* (Indianapolis: Bierce Associates, Inc., 1983), p. 28.

7
What Is Everyday Faith?

Jesus said, "Come to me, all who labor and are heavy laden, and I will give you rest" (Matt. 11:28). He also said, "Go and I will be with you."

Faith is the relationship with God the Father through Jesus Christ, the Son. It is the gift of salvation and the expectation that that salvation will make a difference in our lives. Faith is a "coming home to God" with our frustrations, worries, and faded dreams in anticipation of promised rest. And it is the plunging into the world knowing He is with us. God "tabernacles/tents with us" so we can be at home with God on our journey. *Everyday* faith is coming "home" and staying there . . . everyday. And it is going forth knowing our home is in the tabernacling presence of God who journeys with us.

Everyday faith is hearing God's words to us: "Come, rest in me when you become anxious or nervous or unable to cope with life's demands. Become a trusting child again, and let me Father you."

Everyday faith is hope, hope that "can jump the boundaries or limits, scale the walls of imprisonment, and help the human spirit soar a little closer to God."[1]

What is everyday faith? Please allow us definition with poetic prose.

Everyday faith is:

- love and faith blended together, stillness and action, peace and passion, gift and expectation.
- praying constantly and entering the "stream of silence amidst the noise of life."
- spending quiet time alone with God, and waiting to hear His whispers in the echoes of a busy world.
- finding a divine purpose even in the most routine and unsatisfying tasks.
- holding God in mind every minute of every day, even when other thoughts compete for attention.
- asking God to help us set our priorities and to help us keep them.
- walking through the vegetable gardens and flower beds of our lives and finding there ample reason for praise.
- loving another, not for what he is but for what, in Christ, he can become.
- committing ourselves daily to God, family, friends, church, community, and to the world around us.
- spending time with family and friends and allowing Christ to be the center of each treasured relationship.
- viewing every day of life as a precious gift from God.
- seeing the fingerprints of God's touch on every moment of our lives, always assured that God loves us, guides us, and fully understands us.
- feeling God's heartbeat resonating in our own hearts.
- allowing ourselves to rest, to go for long walks, to bicycle over mountains, to visit our "meditation chairs," even when unfinished work calls to us. It is hearing again Christ's urgings: "Come away . . . and rest a while" (Mark 6:31).
- staying close to God even when He seems so far away.
- knowing that God walks beside us in our loneliness, our illness, our homesickness, and our bereavement, even when we see only one set of footprints in the sand.

• living the Truth instead of lies.

• knowing that God cries with us, and for us, when we lose someone we dearly love.

• asking for daily forgiveness, both for confessed sins and for sins forgotten.

• being forgiven by God, forgiving others, and forgiving ourselves.

• parenting our children with grace, in grace, and always in Christ.

• being faithful to the spouse with whom we are in covenant.

• studying the Scriptures even when our eyes burn from exhaustion and overwork.

• putting aside our boredom and waiting on tiptoe for God in anticipation of discovery.

• giving money and possessions their proper place in our lives.

• choosing right over wrong, striving to be morally pure, living with integrity, and providing a strong, faithful witness to others.

• choosing a vocation and life-style that honors God and pleases God, whether bus driver, homemaker, or theologian.

• telling society it will not break our human spirits and opting for a "style of life" over a "style of death."

Finally, everyday faith is "the assurance of things hoped for, the conviction of things not seen" (Heb. 11:1).

What is everyday faith?

Everyday faith is Truth and Trust personified in Jesus Christ.

Can Everyday Faith Make a Difference In Our Stress-filled Lives?

Yes.

Everyday faith made a difference in Judy Hamilton's life. A wife, mother, and teacher from Washington, West Virginia, Judy underwent the surgical removal of a cancerous breast. Six long months of chemotherapy treatments made her bald, nauseated, unable to eat or drink, and deeply depressed.

"I tried to pray, but I couldn't decide if God was really hearing me," she remembered. "But . . . Romans 8:26 [told me] that the Holy Spirit prays for us when we are unable to make our feelings known to God. . . . the Holy Spirit interceded for me. When I was at my lowest, the Lord Jesus gave me the assurance I needed."[2]

When Judy began to recuperate from the devastating effects of chemotherapy, she received more bad news. Her remaining breast also needed to be removed. More surgery, more treatments.

Again Judy placed her hope in God. "God guarantees us," she could write, "that even though we are pressed on every side by troubles, we will be safe if we live in Christ. This . . . [has] given me strength and hope for the future."[3]

Everyday faith made a difference to Linda Hardesty, a Columbus, Ohio, wife and mother of three.

Linda was a battered wife. Her husband first beat her when she was seven months pregnant. After an argument, he pushed her out the front door and threw most of her clothes on top of her. Before their marriage ended, some seven years later, he beat her often.

She wrote: "Maybe [God] heard me when I cried out 'Oh, God! Oh, God!' as I crawled on my stomach to get away from the blows. I know I prayed the day I hid for eight hours under a mattress in our basement closet as I begged not to be found."[4] "Even when we are too weak to have any faith left, He remains faithful to us and will help us (2 Tim. 2:13)."[5]

Louisville's Helen Parker, wife, author, speaker, and retired braille proofreader, also knows about everyday faith. From childhood, Helen had dreamed of being a schoolteacher. But in her senior year of college, having spent four years preparing to teach, the state of Kentucky denied her a teacher's certificate because she had been born blind.

Helen's first reaction was anger, followed by self-pity, then doubt. She wrote: "I wanted to lash out at God for allowing my well-laid plans to go awry, at society for its discrimination against the handicapped, and at myself for the resentment and self-pity that were building up inside of me."[6]

Instead, however, encouraged by her Christian mother, Helen began to pray about the injustice. She called daily on her faith. And her strong faith in God allowed her to pour out her anger and grievances to Him. It helped her discover gifts she had not before known, gifts that would reach out over her lifetime and minister to others.

Can everyday faith make a difference in our lives?

Ask Terry Helwig, a Louisville wife, mother, and author, how her faith granted her the daily strength and courage she needed to survive her father's suicide. He had visited her only shortly before he took a gun and shot himself.

"The news, like a kick to the stomach, took me to my knees," Terry wrote. "Like a boulder, it tried to crush me. It magnified the pain of death, by what seemed to be a thousand times, because my dad did not have to die. He chose to. He chose to slam shut the book of his life. A life I loved very much."

Terry drew heavily on her faith in the days that followed. And it sustained her.

"Sometimes at night when my pillow is wet from crying,
. . . it is then that I feel God's arms around me. It is then He
assures me that His strength is my strength. It is then He
reminds me that He is never any farther away than a
prayer."[8]

If everyday faith can give us the strength and courage to
cope with cancer, abuse, prejudice, and suicide, how much
more can it help us cope with the everyday, ordinary hassles
of life! Truly, everyday faith gives us the necessary tools to
combat the stress and trials of the everyday.

God's Wonderful Surprise

Having everyday faith is like climbing a staircase. We
don't arrive at the top stair overnight. But we take it step by
step. With each step we grow in and build up our faith,
moving one stair at a time closer to Him, becoming daily
more centered in Christ.

In close relationship with God, daily harassments don't
fluster us as much. Sometimes we don't allow them to fluster
us at all. They come less like floods that threaten to uproot
us and more like stubborn cows who step across our train
track and detain us temporarily.

God's wonderful surprise to us, in our discovery of an
everyday faith, is this: While everyday faith will not remove
all the stubborn cows from our tracks, it *will* change the way
we respond to those cows! *Staying close to Jesus Christ hourly will
drastically transform the way we respond to everyday stress.*

Responding to Everyday Stress with Everyday Faith

Of course, Steven Carreker and Denise George don't pre-
tend to have all the answers into the mysteries of faith. We,
too, are mere travelers on faith's long journey. But based on
what everyday faith has done—and is doing—in our lives,

please allow us, in the next chapters, to suggest how an active everyday faith might help you respond to active everyday stress.

Will the way you respond to everyday stress through everyday faith make a difference in your life? We believe it will.

Notes

1. Henlee Barnette, *Your Freedom to Be Whole* (Philadelphia: The Westminster Press, 1984), p. 31.

2. Judy Hamilton, "Breast Cancer," Compiler Denise George, *When Night Becomes As Day* (Nashville: Broadman Press, 1986), p. 111.

3. Ibid., p. 113.

4. Linda Hardesty, "I Was a Battered Wife," *When Night Becomes As Day,* p. 130.

5. Ibid.

6. Helen Parker, "Blind Prejudice," *When Night Becomes As Day,* p. 143.

7. Terry Helwig, "My Father's Suicide," *When Night Becomes As Day,* p. 165.

8. Ibid., p. 168.

8

What Everyday Faith Can Do for You

We already know what everyday stress can do *to* you. Let us now look at what everyday faith can do *for* you.

I.

We believe an active everyday faith will make a difference to you personally.

As God moves to the center of our being, stress must move to the sidelines. Everyday hassles become more minor irritations than front-line guerrilla warfare. And, while we will still know our share of "blue-collar blues" and "white-collar woes," still get stuck in traffic, feel lonely occasionally, and experience a bad night's sleep, we will be able to see stress in a better perspective. We can better choose to avoid letting minor irritations "nibble us to death."

For instance, we will be able to look at the scratches on our new car as an opportunity to behave in a Christlike manner to the one who recklessly put them there. The cigar-smoking, too-demanding boss will challenge us to greater heights of loving and praying for our "enemies." The first argument with our new bride will call us to new meanings of compromise and commitment. And the longed-for newborn babe who sleeps all day and cries all night . . . well, that's a tough one! Perhaps we will look at child rearing more in light of the eternal than the temporary.

We've discovered that resting in Christ daily helps dissolve previous stressful fears about growing up and growing older. God promises to stay close beside us and to guide us in all life's moments and in all life's stages. We can look to Him as a child looks to a parent, to meet our needs for survival and safety.

Confident in Christ, we can reach out to others in greater vulnerability and honesty. In doing so, we will find that people more readily reach back to us, helping to fill our needs for love and belonging.

Realizing that Christ loves us and, with His life, proved that love, we will have heightened regard, love, and acceptance for ourselves.

And daily, as we move closer into His presence, we will begin to experience more "peak" mystical moments of happiness and wonderment as He sends us rare insights into life and beyond.

Practicing His presence, we come to depend on Him more for hour-to-hour guidance as we strive to stay within certain limits.

Our new list of priorities will greatly influence the way we spend and manage our time and money.

We will view our bodies not just as "our" bodies but as "temple[s] of the Holy Spirit" (1 Cor. 6:19). We will treat them more kindly and with greater respect, feeding them better, seeking to keep them safe and away from high-risk situations, saying no to harmful drugs and chemicals, resting them when they tire, buckling them into car seats, and exercising them to keep them toned.

As we become more keenly aware of Christ's gentle and loving discipline, we will put greater value on our Christian integrity and morality. We will no longer live only for ourselves but for God and others. We will be concerned about the faithful witness we give to others. We will take to heart

Paul's advice to the Colossian church: "Whatever you do, in word or deed, do everything in the name of the Lord Jesus" (Col. 3:17).

All in all, our daily faith will change our everydays. Billy Graham wrote: "The day begins with a sunrise; but the sun sets, the shadows gather, and that calendar day is crossed out, never to appear again. We will never be able to repeat today. It is gone forever."[1]

You and I can more graciously close our everydays knowing we spent them well, that we filled them with praise and thanksgiving, with prayer and meditation, and with goodness and joy that reached up to God, out to others, and back to us. When the sun sets and the shadows gather, when the calendar day is crossed out, we will be the richer for having held within us, for those unrepeatable twenty-four hours, the beauty of renewed faith—the one more step we climbed up the spiritual staircase.

II.

We believe active everyday faith will make a difference to you spiritually.

Prayer, worship, study, and ministry take on new meaning when we give God hours instead of minutes.

Prayer

Prayer produces an affinity with God, a close and spontaneous love and relationship. The emptiness and loneliness that gnawed at us begins to ease when we feel comfortable enough to confide these to God. Prayer is bringing your whole self honestly into the presence of God. Such are the Psalms which John Calvin called "the anatomy of all parts of the soul." Prayer becomes a time of deep intimacy and celebration. In our prayerful seeking, God presents us a new dimension and perspective into life. Prayer enables us to respond with greater wisdom and delicacy to highly stressful situations. When we pray, we learn better how to pray. We appreciate more the Spirit within us that never ceases to pray for us (Rom. 8:26).

In prayer we search, question, and affirm what we believe. We are given the freedom to ask God anything, which helps our faith to grow.

Worship

It's hard to know where prayer ends and worship begins. Worship is most honestly entered into through the door of prayer.

We believe public worship is important. We need the formal service of worship, the "saying out loud" of our everyday faith with other believers and the Christian fellowship it invokes. But in everyday faith, we've found private, personal worship essential.

Our private worship swells out of prayer; and because it is personal and private, it remains informal. Personal worship takes shape as we become aware of God, who is always present to us. In these encounters with the Divine, we are awed by His grandeur, and we tell Him. We are amazed at His interest in us, and we thank Him. We praise. We give thanks. We confess the sins we know He already knows even before we commit them. We meditate on Scripture, and we attempt to understand how it applies to us. We conclude our private worship reassured that His faithfulness to us will enable us to be faithful to Him.

In everyday faith, we are learning that the "prayer closet" is becoming the necessary cathedral for worship.

Loving God with Our Minds

Faith study (loving God with our minds) opens the doors to the world God has created and to the expectations that He holds for us, His followers. In order for our everyday faith to have more influence over us than our everyday stress, we study the faith, and we learn from it.

What do we study? We study Scripture, the history of the church, and contemporary responses to contemporary culture.

We study Scripture because it is the world of God given to us. It leads us to salvation and abundant life.

We study church history to see how the church has responded to Christ over the years. We study to know how our denomination came into being and why we chose that particular expression of faith. We study to learn how the giants of faith lived faithfully over the centuries and how we can follow their time-proven examples.

Most of all, we study because Jesus Christ bids us to study, to love Him with our minds. We study the faith so we can learn more about the faith, so the faith can grow into belief, the belief can extend into value, and, at last, the belief can turn into faith behavior. We study the faith because belief makes a difference in behavior.

Reaching Out in Ministry

In faith, stress turns to energy, energy that can be used to bless others.

As followers of Christ, we are called on to put our everyday faith into everyday energy—ministry. In ministry, we are called on to give. "Love your neighbor" (Mark 12:31), "Whatsoever you wish that men would do to you, do so to them" (Matt. 7:12), "Through love be servants of all" (Gal.

5:13) are all mandates from God for active ministry. We become His eyes, His ears, and His hands. We minister when we encourage the despondent, hold the suicidal, visit the sick, help the elderly, teach the seeker, and play with the child. Ministry to others is everyday faith in action.

Everyday faith is also receiving ministry from others. Christ often ministers to us through church, family, friends, and community "people packages." Receiving ministry can be more difficult for us, but, in doing so, we extend the privilege of active everyday ministry to another.

Receiving ministry means accepting the strong, loving arms that God wraps around us through a friend.

III.

How hard it is for us to write to Christians about their money! It's like entering a field of explosive mines. Barefoot. If one enters at all, one must do so on tiptoe and with extreme caution.

So we take off our shoes and, on tiptoe, we enter.

We believe active everyday faith will make a difference to you financially.

Our attitudes about money and possessions have begun to change. Money has become less a way to accumulate possessions and more a way to enable ministry. The importance of owning things diminishes as we see how money can enable ministry.

We are trying harder to pull free from the possessions that can so powerfully possess us. We are beginning to laugh at crazy ad campaigns that jingle us to buy the latest and greatest "can't-live-without" electric potato peeler. Contentment with what we have is slowly replacing the desire to splurge on the pink plastic poodles of life we didn't need in the first place.

Becoming Christ centered instead of stress centered might even mean giving up some income.

"Income isn't everything if your life-style is bringing you hassles instead of happiness," claims the American Institute of Stress. They suggest: "Take inventory and ask youself if more family time wouldn't make you happier than a larger home that would mean more work, more commuting time to work, and more bills."[2]

Becoming God centered keeps us from thinking too much about *having* money and more about *giving money away.* It keeps us always striving for a more simple, more contented life-style. "'Tis a *gift* to be simple," sang the Shakers. It's not easy, however, to live simply in our unsimple society. But we're discovering that a more simple life-style brings with it greater freedom from stress and greater dependence on God.

IV.

We believe active everyday faith will make a difference to you in your relationships.

Relationship is God's grace gift for our stressful aloneness. People show us how diverse God is. They compose a mural of the many faces of God. Everyday faith makes us respond to people, even strangers, much more positively. It gives us an inner radiance that invites and strengthens relationship with others. Being centered in Christ, we will respond to each other more naturally, more honestly, and with greater love and kindness (Eph. 4:32). In Christ, we call out the very best in one another.

People Packages

People come to us in different packages.

People packages of our past, our ancestors, give us far more than genetic transference. They give us the very elements of our everyday faith. Long journeys into our past help us travel many miles of memories, both positive and negative. Coming to terms and to peace with our past brings relief in itself. We learn to let go of painful memories, to forgive people in our past, and to treasure more the rich memories. Coming home to our past is one of God's best gifts for our everyday faith.

Family is another people package. It's natural to be family. It is nice to be friends with family. But family can be difficult simply because its members are so diverse. We are many things to many people: child-sibling-spouse-parent-in-law-grandparent. It is no secret that different ages and energy levels can cause multifaceted family stress.

Everyday faith in the family is rooted in submission to Jesus Christ. This submission to Christ can convert and refine us into the attitude of mutual submission to our family members. Hour after hour of grinding out ball bearings at a factory or heaping loads of dirty laundry into the washer day after day is an act of Christ's love and submission, for we make ball bearings and wash dirty laundry not only for our spouses or children or elderly parents, but we do these life tasks for Christ, in humble submission to Him because we love Him. This type of divine submission, as hard as it can be, enriches the family. It stems from everyday faith, and it equips us for the beautiful blessings of everyday family! Family covenant, based on mutual Christlike submission and trust, offers us sanctuary, home, for the day-by-day maturing and growing of our everyday faith.

Human beings need this covenant sanctuary and system of support and affirmation. It protects and enriches us, especially our youngest members.

Harold Warlick wrote: "Parents and children . . . can come

together to develop a system of tremendous personal support and affirmation to shield against many of the hurts in life. . . . [This] system . . . reassures the person that he or she can survive stress."[3]

Our children need us in family if they are to reach a healthy development of personhood.

Dr. Kathryn Chapman states it beautifully: "Significant adults, persons who relate to children with love and concern, join God in the sacred task of creation."[4]

She also admitted that in this "creating," part of *our* task is "to be in step with God's timing, a creative pacing divinely led."[5]

Thus, we are to be faithful to the task of everyday faith.

Local church congregations is a third people package that rises right out of the heart of our everyday faith. We do not choose our past, our biological family. Most often we do not choose our community. As adults, however, we can choose the local church with whom we make covenant. The church we choose will have much to do with sustaining our everyday faith.

Our everyday faith offers a fourth people package of *support groups.* Intimacy. Struggle. Trust. Confession. Sharing. Vulnerability. These call for support. Support often happens best in small groups. Small-group dynamics has become one of the most significant social developments in the last half of the twentieth century.

Support groups offer the security of confidentiality and limits. In a small group, we are accountable to only a few people, and there, for a brief time, we are concerned with the needs and gifts of these few people. Small groups may be the best community for the rich struggle of deep, honest, searching everyday faith. It was in small groups that Jesus gave everyday faith to the first apostles. In support groups, everyday faith leaps its highest and grows its deepest.

Everyday faith allows us involvement in many relationships, as it enables us to see people as significant. It expands on the old question of "Who is my neighbor?" with "Where is my neighbor?" and "How is my neighbor?"

Everyday faith reminds us that Christ-centered presence with another person is truly a rare gift of God.

Forgiveness

Relationships also include forgiveness. Even with everyday faith we continue to fail, to make mistakes, to sin. Fortunately, Christ offers us forgiveness and freedom from our failings.

Forgiveness is the ink with which the New Testament is written, the evidence of God's perpetual and eternal grace. Forgiveness is the seal of His constant abiding with us, the "again" of His invitation and call.

Forgiveness means honest confession and repentance to God and to those we have wronged. It means giving up the wrong and striving to make that wrong right again, even when we do so at uncomfortable, and often embarrassing, risk to ourselves. Experiencing God's rich forgiveness means hearing again Jesus' instruction to the woman taken in the act of adultery: "Go, and do not sin again" (John 8:11).

So, as forgiven ones, we repent, we confess, we tell the truth, and we try to live right. We honestly strive to avoid sinning.

That God forgives us, we need little convincing. He does. That we are to forgive others, we need little prompting, though we may find it very difficult to accomplish. Forgiveness is often a small-step-by-small-step process. That we are to forgive ourselves is the difficult task. How often we accept His forgiveness, yet we will not forgive ourselves and let go of our guilt. Perhaps we best celebrate God's grace by forgiving ourselves, by living as forgiven ones because we belong to the One who died to forgive us.

* * *

We invite you to take the "everyday faith test" and then to continue with us through another chapter as we suggest practical day-to-day exercises toward an active everyday faith.

Notes

1. Billy Graham, "Rushing Toward the End," *Decision,* Sept. 1987, p. 2.
2. "39 Ways to De-stress Your Home Life," *Prevention Magazine,* Vol. 39, No. 9, Sept. 1987, p. 83.
3. Warlick, *Conquering Loneliness,* p. 54.
4. Kathryn Chapman, *When Children Suffer,* Ed. Andrew D. Lester (Philadelphia: The Westminster Press, 1987), p. 43.
5. Ibid.

My Everyday Faith Test

Mark the following questions with "true" or "false."

General Faith Areas	True	False
1. I don't have to work hard at my everyday faith.	____	____
2. I'm very confident in my everyday faith.	____	____
3. I can talk with ease about my everyday faith.	____	____
4. I'm content with the exercises of my everyday faith.	____	____
5. My everyday faith relieves my everyday stress.	____	____
6. My everyday faith is very dear to me.	____	____
7. I can easily share my everyday faith.	____	____
8. I know what I believe.	____	____
9. My public religion is a continuation of my everyday faith.	____	____
10. My family can explain the dynamics of my everyday faith.		

Prayer

1. I pray regularly for other people.	____	____
2. I have a regular personal devotion time.	____	____
3. I'm able to pray for God's will in my life.	____	____
4. My constant gratitude prevents me from taking God for granted.	____	____
5. I pray with my family with honesty and with significant meaning.	____	____
6. I'm confident about my ability to listen to God.	____	____
7. I sense that the Holy Spirit is praying for me.	____	____
8. I have a prayer partner with whom I pray.	____	____

Worship

1. I'm very open about praising God.	____	____
2. Public worship events evoke my personal commitment.	____	____
3. What I believe makes a difference in how I behave.	____	____
4. I celebrate His abounding grace as I act out His call.	____	____

Study of the Faith

1. I'm satisfied with my Scripture study habits.	____	____
2. I have read or intend to read one or more of the Christian classics.	____	____
3. I memorize Scripture.	____	____

4. I treasure Scripture.   ___ ___
5. I can teach another how to study Scripture.   ___ ___

Relationships

1. I do not know of anyone I need to forgive.   ___ ___
2. I have come to peace with my past.   ___ ___
3. I am friends with my family members.   ___ ___
4. I am active in my local church.   ___ ___
5. I give myself to community.   ___ ___
6. My local church strengthens my everyday faith. ___ ___
8. I have a support group for faith dialogue.   ___ ___

Ministry

1. I have clarified my spiritual gifts.   ___ ___
2. I allow other people to minister to me.   ___ ___
3. I am perceptive of needs around me and in the
   world.   ___ ___
4. I minister to other people.   ___ ___
5. I use my spiritual gifts in ministry.   ___ ___

Resource Management

1. I use my time wisely.   ___ ___
2. I have the faith to rest.   ___ ___
3. I feel good about my money management.   ___ ___
4. I am a disciplined consumer.   ___ ___
5. I'd rather invest my money in people than in
   things.   ___ ___

Forgiveness

1. I feel no ongoing resentment toward anyone.   ___ ___
2. I believe God has forgiven me.   ___ ___
3. I have forgiven myself of my faults and sins.

   This questionnaire is designed to help you measure how you feel about
your everyday faith. It will also help you identify the category of everyday
faith in which you would like to grow.
   Each "false" answer can be an area of everyday faith in which you may
choose to grow. Each "true" answer provides areas which are helpful
though not all necessarily indicate a need for growth.

Section IV
Hope for Your
Future Everydays

Therefore be imitators of God,
as beloved children.
And walk in love,
as Christ loved us
and gave himself up for us.

Ephesians 5:1-2

9

101 Faithful Ways to De-stress Your Life

As Christians, most of us want to de-stress as much of the distress in our lives as possible. We are finding these faith exercises helpful to us in relieving much of our everyday stress. We hope you will find them helpful, too.

As you read, please circle the faith exercises you already do. Mark with an *x* the ones you would like to do, the ones that would blend most naturally into your daily, weekly, or monthly schedule.

We hope you will keep the list handy and gradually incorporate those exercises meaningful to you into your day. It's not important that you try to include all 101! That might be impossible.

(When you finish each category, use a separate sheet of paper to record your own faithful, stress-relieving exercises.)

How can you, how can we, faithfully de-stress much of the distress in our lives?

Through Prayer

1. Pray daily. Open your day with prayer. Close your day with prayer.

2. Pray all during the day, even if your prayer is only one sentence long. "Pray without ceasing," Paul urged (1 Thess. 5:17, KJV).

3. Try praying with mental images instead of words.

"The fewer words the better prayer," believed Martin Luther.

4. Schedule certain regular times of prayer and, if possible, protect those times from interruption.

5. Gradually lengthen your prayer time, if only by a few extra minutes a week.

6. On days you don't feel like praying, pray the Lord's Prayer or pray printed prayers that others have prayed.

7. Pray the Scriptures. On days when your own prayerful words won't easily come, turn to the Psalms and pray the beautiful words of the psalmist.

8. Select a prayer partner. Set a specific time to pray separately for each other.

9. Schedule time with your prayer partner to pray together.

10. Become prayer partners with your family, and make regular "prayer appointments" to pray together.

11. Start or join a prayer group that meets once a week in your church or community.

12. Start a prayer group in your home. Invite special friends to gather for mutual prayer, support, and encouragement.

13. Always look for new and unusual places to pray. Pray while you scramble eggs, mow the yard, fold the laundry, or wait at a traffic light.

14. Be on the lookout for new ways to pray. For instance, pray "open-eyed prayers" as you drive your children to school. Let them hear you pray for their day, their safety, their teachers, and their fellow classmates. Invite them to pray open-eyed with you.

15. When you pray with your child, match the prayer with his age. For example: invite the child to draw a prayer

with crayons. If he sketches Grandmother, then stop a moment and pray together for Grandmother.

16. Have family "walk" prayers. While you walk, point out God's creation, and thank God aloud for the caterpillar that crosses the path or for the rainbow that graces the sky.

17. Create "play" prayers. Let your children choose a favorite Bible story, and then let each member of the family act it out.

18. Have family "sing" prayers. Make up a tune to your favorite Scripture verse and sing it together. Or make up your own words to a familiar tune. Or sing the Psalms as the early church did.[1]

19. Involve your family, prayer group, or Sunday School class in sentence prayers. Begin with a period of silence, and then invite one person at a time to pray a prayerful sentence.

20. Invite your family members to pray silent prayers. Gather in the family room or around the kitchen table, and sit together in silence for a few minutes each day.

21. Write your prayers in a notebook. Keep this "prayer journal" for one month, and then reflect back on it. Discover how creatively God answered your prayers.

22. Share your prayer journal with your prayer partner or a friend.

23. Give your prayer journal as a gift to the person you have held most often in prayer.

24. Mail a prayer a day. Write a prayer of gratitude to a person you appreciate. Write a prayer of encouragement to someone undergoing a crisis. Write a prayer of support to a person struggling to make a difficult decision. Write an "I'm-praying-for-you" prayer to someone who is lonely or homesick.

25. Write a "booklet" of prayers to your child as she grows up. Include a personal prayer to mark each special

occasion in her life. Give her this prayer remembrance. She will thank you for surrounding her with a lifetime of prayer.

26. In your regular correspondence, jot a prayer of blessing at the end of your letter. A favorite of ours is the ancient Hebrew blessing (Num. 6:24-26): "The Lord bless you and keep you:/The Lord make his face to shine/upon you, and be gracious to you:/The Lord lift up his countenance upon/you, and give you peace."

What a gift of blessing you will leave your readers to ponder, to reflect upon, and to carry with them all during the day.

27. Pray daily for those you know and love, as well as those you've not yet come to know and love. Pray even for those who mistreat you.

28. Tell the people for whom you are praying that you're praying for them.

29. If possible, take a half-day, half-hour, or even a five-minute prayer vacation. Walk through the woods and pray. Choose your favorite garden spot and pray. Relax in your "meditation" chair and pray.

30. Try to arrange a prayer retreat for just yourself, or for your family, too. Monasteries, convents, state parks, and retreat centers can offer solitude and peaceful quiet for a few days of retreating with God.

31. Find a comfortable seat in a nearby shopping mall, and pray "thought prayers" for everyone who passes by you.

32. Breathe a silent prayer for each of the co-workers you greet daily in your job.

33. At regular intervals (perhaps every day, week, or month), ask God to direct your daily, weekly, or monthly goal setting.

34. Sit quietly during your prayer time and allow God to minister to you.

35. Speak less to God, and let God speak more to you.

36. Pray constantly for the desire to pray constantly.

Through Worship

37. Worship God by daily reading a psalm.

38. Write your own psalm of praise and thanksgiving.

39. Throughout your day, sing or hum your favorite hymns of praise.

40. Seek to discover the child in you who looks at God's creation with wonderment.

41. List all the words you can think of to describe God.

42. Keep a devotional journal of your most memorable worship moments and events.

43. Tell God often: "I love You."

44. Worship regularly with fellow Christians and enter your responses in a journal.

45. Support your chosen congregation with your time, money, thoughts, and energy.

46. Become a member of your church's worship committee, and have active input into the order of worship.

47. Find the place you can best worship alone. Is it a favorite fishing hole, or backyard porch swing, or community rose garden? Visit it and worship as often as you can.

48. Plan regular worship services in your home with your family. Include singing, praying, and Scripture reading. Encourage each member to actively participate.

49. Plan family worship services to celebrate holidays and special occasions, such as Thanksgiving, Christmas, Easter, birthdays, adoption days, anniversaries, and "firsts" days.

Through Study

50. Read your Bible every day, if only a few verses.

51. Start at Genesis 1, and, over one year's time, read your Bible all the way through.

52. Memorize the Bible verses you hold dear.

53. Begin a Bible study group in your home, church, or community. Meet once a week to read, study, and discuss Scripture together.

54. Study with disciplined energy your favorite book in the Bible, and become an expert on it.

55. Offer to teach your favorite Bible book to your Sunday School class or Bible study group.

56. Start a "Matthew, Mark, Luke, and lunch" group. How? Once a month, pack a lunch to eat with a few good friends, and together discuss a chosen portion of the Gospels.

57. Read the classics of faith such as Bunyan's *The Pilgrim's Progress,* Brother Lawrence's *Practice of the Presence of God,* Thomas á Kempis's *Imitation of Christ,* or J. Baillie's *Diary of Private Prayer,* etc.

58. Teach yourself and your children the Lord's Prayer, the Apostle's Creed, the Books of the Bible, etc.

59. Trace your faith roots. Who mothered and fathered you into the faith? To what denominations did your ancestors belong? Why have you chosen your particular denomination of faith? Return in memory often to your childhood faith and be thankful for all those who planted faith's seed in you.

60. Strive to be open to those whose theology differs from yours. Seek prayerful understanding into their beliefs. Pray for reconciliation when denominational differences cause dispute.

Through Ministry to Others

61. List your spiritual gifts. Ask God for the privilege of using your gifts in His work.

62. Take your God-given gifts seriously. After you discover them, learn about them, polish them, and seek always to use them for God.

63. Identify the five most pressing needs around you, and work actively to meet those needs.

64. Schedule blocks of time in your calendar to reach out in ministry to another. Do you have an hour to grocery shop for an elderly man in your community? Can you give a day to play with a child in a nearby housing project? Do you have a few minutes to write a check for a church food pantry for the hungry in your neighborhood? Can you take half a day and help your pastor or other staff member deliver food baskets at Christmas?

65. Find a ministry partner, or pastor, or form a ministry team. Work together and encourage each other in reaching out to others around you who are in need.

66. Seek new and creative ways to minister through your words and actions. Join a softball team, and, with encouraging words, help build the self-esteem of inner-city youngsters. Paste braille labels on baby food jars for the blind mother who lives down the street. Plan a picnic for a family who has little money and no transportation. Find ways to minister to your co-workers, your neighbors, and even your minister. Are you a dentist, or doctor, or lawyer? Donate hours of service to those who need it and can't afford it. There are no limits to ways to minister creatively.

Through Ministry to Yourself

67. As you plan creative ways to minister to others, remember to also minister to yourself.

68. Strive to become your own best friend. Listen to yourself and hear what you are saying. Take care of your body and furnish its needs. Befriend yourself, accept yourself, and love more deeply the One who lives within you.

69. Celebrate the unique person God created you to be.

70. Become aware of the gifts God has given you. Claim them, use them, enjoy them, and revel in them.

71. Choose your stress battles.

72. Allow yourself times of solitude and quiet, celebration and satisfaction, merriment and play. Laugh . . . a lot.

73. Delight yourself in God's good creation. The Artist gave you a rainbow of natural colors to enjoy, the sounds of laughing children rolling down a grassy hill, and the soft fur of kittens to stroke. See, hear, and stroke God's work of art.

74. Give yourself time and permission to exercise your body, educate your mind, enjoy your family, and stimulate your interests.

75. Take vacations, whether brief or long, from your regular work load. Give yourself the right to rest.

76. Be gentle and more loving with yourself. Refrain from harsh self-criticism. Tell yourself at least once daily that God loves you, accepts you, and forgives you.

77. Schedule your day's work and activities (that *can* be scheduled) to allow yourself some breathing room.

78. Give yourself the gift of a more simple life-style, and enjoy the freedom that the "lack of things" can bring.

79. Go through your home and sort out all the clothes, furniture, appliances, and general household goods you can

live without. Give these things to those who truly need them.

80. Do not allow your money to hold ultimate power over you; it is your servant and not your master.

81. Give as much of your money away as you can afford to give. Let money enable ministry to others. Let money be "the servant." Let it *work* for you and for others.

82. As you minister to yourself, remember to be kind to yourself, for you belong to Christ who is Kindness Incarnate.

Through Relationship

83. Strive to develop and grow in your first and most important relationship—your relationship with God.

84. Keep all your relationships good, pure, honest, mutually uplifting, and *always centered in Christ.*

85. Make time for, and spend time with, those people you love. Keep in touch with good friends from your past. (You can't make old friends!)

86. Look for the image of God in all people.

87. Share at least one meal a day with your family. The meal need not be elaborate. You need not even sit around the table. You can roast hot dogs over a fire, eat peanut-butter-and-jelly sandwiches on the playground, or eat "McBurgers" in your car. But eat together, be together, and talk together. For all three fulfill basic human family needs.

88. In family, pray together and play together. Build up each other. Be thankful for each other. Love each other deeply.

89. Talk to your children about all those who came before them. Routinely, pull out the family photo album and let your children ask about, learn about, and come to care deeply about their ancestors. Give them these unforgot-

ten roots, so they may grow stronger from the knowledge and pass the faith heritage on to those who come after them.

90. Get together with family members and friends and dream your dreams. Share your stress with those you love and trust.

91. Spend both "quality" and "quantity" time with your family. In doing so, you will let your family members know you love them, care about them, and enjoy their presence.

92. Make an effort to know others, especially your neighbors. Reach out to them in kindness whenever you can. Live peaceably with them.

93. Initiate relationships with others. Some psychologists estimate that at least 50 percent of Americans are lonely. Love the lonely and, in Christlike ways, befriend them.

94. In your family, church, vocation, and community, do your portion of the work, and take your part of the responsibilities. Be careful that your chosen jobs aren't imposed on another so that others must do more than their share or routinely cover for you.

95. Strive to uplift, affirm, encourage, approve, and commend all those you meet.

Through Forgiveness

96. Take some time to yourself and list all the sins in your life for which you wish God's forgiveness. Present these to God in confessions and repentance. Ask Him to forgive you. Thank Him for His willingness to forgive you. And thank Him for forgiving you.

97. After God has forgiven you, use the same list, and write down all those who have sinned against you. All those who have used you, lied to you, cheated you, or abused you. Then, asking God's help, forgive them, and allow God to

take away the anger and hurt and disappointment you feel for them.

98. This step is the hardest, most uncomfortable, and most embarrassing. On your list, write down all the times you have used, lied to, cheated, and abused another person. List all those you resent, are jealous of, or hold a grudge against. Then, praying for God's courage, go to each person and ask his or her forgiveness.

99. Use the same list and, sin by sin, ask God to help you to forgive yourself. Then celebrate the "letting go" of these sins. Inhale the fresh air of inner cleansing and new energy!

100. Tear up the list and throw it away. God has forgiven you. You have forgiven others. You have forgiven yourself.

101. And go in peace.

Note

1. Denise George, "How to: Turn Young Energy Into Prayer Power," *Guideposts*, Jan. 1988, pp. 18-19.

10
The Surprising Results
of Everyday Faith

"Great faith exercises there, all 101 of them," you might be thinking right now. "But can we really *use* them in our hectic, everyday, stress-filled life?"

Good question! It has been our question, too. And we have discovered that the answer is yes!

How can everyday exercises of faith make a difference to the way you respond to everyday exercises of stress?

Life's Everyday Stressful Situation #1

Crunch! You back out of the grocery store parking lot, directly into a woman's new red Mercedes. Your seven-year-old Plymouth Satellite is barely scratched. Her car, however, sports a deep, ugly dent. You take a deep breath, silently wish she had been driving a Volkswagen Rabbit, and mentally prepare yourself for the worst. The worst happens. The woman lunges at your car, beats the hood with her fists, and berates you with hard-hitting, angry words.

Everyday stress tells you to:

Hit her back with angry words, tell her "where to get off," and then drive off!

Everyday faith allows you to:

Keep your cool. Listen quietly to her, and after she calms down, apologize for smashing her fender. No doubt, your unexpected tenderness toward her will reach out to her in ministry, whether she knows it or not. Your Christlike example will guard you from excess stress and speak volumes to her—and all the others like her that you will, throughout your lifetime, probably also "run into."

(Caught in a similar situation, my friend Terry Helwig went one step further. Everyday faith allowed her to send a bouquet of purple iris and yellow tulips to the angry, hood-beating woman she ran into.)

Everyday faith exercises:

(See previous chapter, numbers: 27, 66, 71, 86, 92, and 95.)

Scriptural reminder of faith:

Romans 8:28: God works in *all* things for His good purpose. Even smashed Mercedes fenders.

Life's Everyday Stressful Situation #2

You've had a long, hard day at the office. You pick up the kids from school, stop by the grocery for a chicken, and finally arrive home. Your feet hurt, and your kids are hungry and whining. You just want to take off your shoes, put your feet up, and collapse.

When you open the front door, however, you are greeted with disaster. The cat has knocked over your tree-size house plant, and your cream-colored carpet is covered with dirt.

Everyday stress tells you to:

Scream at the kids and the cat. Lock yourself in your bedroom for the next hour and cry.

Everyday faith allows you to:

Take off your shoes, hand the kids a box of cheese and crackers, put your tired feet up, and take a fifteen-minute prayer rest. The chicken can wait. The carpet can wait. You are choosing, at this particular moment, not to be stressed.

Everyday faith exercises:

(See #2, 29, 34, 35, 37, 39, 41, 43, 47, 50, 67, 68, 69, 71, 72, 75, 77, and 82.)

Scriptural reminder of faith:

Luke 18:1: When stress threatens to overwhelm you, don't lose heart. Stop and pray. Take a prayer vacation, and when you again open your eyes, you'll probably view the whining children, the waiting chicken, and the soiled carpet with new perspective!

Life's Everyday Stressful Situation #3

You are a single parent, and your teenage son has become overly rebellious. You don't like the boys he runs with. He no longer obeys your house rules, and you feel you just can't handle the situation alone anymore. You have Christian friends who love you and would offer their help, but you are embarrassed that you can't handle the problem alone.

Everyday stress tells you to:

Be "strong" and try, single-handedly, to help your son. Wring your hands and worry about him. Feel isolated and alone and hopeless.

Everyday faith allows you to understand that:

It's OK to need others. Reach out to your friends for help. Share your concerns with loving Christian people who would come together, support you, and pray with you. Let them help you and your son. Let them recommend a pastoral counselor to help you, too. Don't try to carry the burden of stress alone. Share the stress, and let others minister to you through love and prayer.

Everyday faith exercises:

(See #1, 2, 3, 4, 6, 7, 8, 9, 10, 11, 12, 20, 21, 22, 23, 25, 27, 28, 29, 30, 34, 35, 36, 37, 38, 41, 42, 43, 44, 45, 47, 50, 52, 53, 56, 65, 67, 69, 72, 83, 85, 86, 87, 88, 89, 90, 91, 93, and 97.)

Scriptural reminder of faith:

Isaiah 40:1-2: In our everydays, let us reach out and comfort each other. And let *us* be helped, be encouraged, be comforted by God Himself, as He comes to us with the hands, wisdom, and arms of Christian friends.

Life's Everyday Stressful Situation #4

You are lonely. Your spouse died a few years ago, and your grown children have families of their own and live in different states. Oh, you have some friends at church and in your neighborhood, but you miss the loving intimacy of spouse and family. You sometimes think no one really loves you or cares deeply about you. You feel sad and lonely most of the time now. You have even wondered if life is worth living at all.

Everyday stress tells you that:

You are all alone in this crowded world of strangers. Go ahead and feel unloved. Mull over it, and think about your loneliness day and night. There's really nothing you can do about loneliness.

Everyday faith allows you to:

Pull closer to God in your loneliness. Know that God loves you and that He went to great lengths one starlit night in Bethlehem to prove that love. Had you been the only living person in the world, God would have made His personal visit to earth just for you. God lives within you. He will not leave you. He will never stop loving you. His love is the most intimate love you could ever experience. In fact, nothing can stop God from loving you, not even the stress of everyday loneliness!

Everyday faith allows you to experience fully God's love, secure in the knowledge that God loves you, as well as to reach out and receive the love of others.

Celebrate God's love and presence through prayer and worship, both alone and with others. Be assured of God's love for you through studying His scriptural promises. Become part of prayer, worship, study, and ministry support groups. You will not only grow in your everyday faith, but the stress of loneliness will ease as you share your faith and yourself in Christ's love with others.

Everyday faith exercises:

(See #1, 2, 3, 4, 5, 6, 7, 8, 9, 11, 12, 13, 21, 22, 26, 31, 34, 35, 37, 38, 40, 41, 42, 43, 44, 45, 46, 50, 51, 52, 53, 54, 55, 56, 57, 59, 61, 62, 63, 64, 65, 66, 67, 68, 69, 70, 72, 73, 74, 83, 85, 90, 92, and 93.)

Scriptural reminder of faith:

Romans 8:35-39: "For I am sure that neither death, nor life, nor angels, nor principalities, nor things present, nor things to come, nor powers, nor height, nor depth, nor anything else in all creation, will be able to separate us from the love of God in Christ Jesus our Lord."

Life's Everyday Stressful Situation #5

Your young children don't seem very interested in praying anymore. They no longer bow their heads, close their eyes, and remain quiet for suppertime grace. Both you and your spouse are faithful pray-ers, and, frankly, you're beginning to worry about your children's attitude toward spiritual things. Peer group pressure and outside activities seem to have offset, somehow, the spiritual influence of your home.

Everyday stress tells you to:

Scold them and make them sit deadly still at suppertime grace. Remember, you're the BOSS. Not them. Teach them to pray whether they like it or not!

Everyday faith allows you to:

Consider their young ages and their need to experience prayer in ways different from yours. Be creative in finding new approaches to make prayer meaningful for your children. For instance, try "open-eyed" prayers at the supper table. During the day, let them draw prayers with crayons or have evening-family-walk prayers or "singing" prayers with you. Strive to make prayer time with your children a fun time of learning and worship. A time of blessing, not a time of stress.

Everyday faith exercises:

(See #10, 12, 14, 15, 16, 17, 18, 19, 20, 24, 25, 28, 30, 31, 37, 38, 39, 41, 48, 49, 50, 51, 52, 53, 58, 59, 83, 85, 86, 87, 88, 89, 90, and 91.)

Scriptural reminder of faith:

Psalm 100: In your family's celebration of faith, teach your children to make joyful noises to God, to sing to Him, to serve Him with their childlike happiness and gladness. To thank Him, to praise Him, to bless His name!

Life's Everyday Stressful Situation #6

In one day, the toilet stops up and pours water all over the bathroom floor, the dishwasher stops washing, and the freezer stops freezing. "This can't really be happening!" you exclaim as you run with your carton of dripping chocolate ice cream across the backyard to your neighbor's freezer.

This is all very stressful. Yet you feel even more stressed when you pay each repairman's neatly itemized bill.

Everyday stress tells you to:

Kick the toilet, dishwasher, and freezer. Then give up, take two aspirin, and go to bed . . . grumbling.

Everyday faith allows you to:

Laugh! (Really?) Why, this is funnier than Laurel and Hardy! "When it rains, it pours" and all that! Anyway, "It couldn't happen to a nicer person!"

You can laugh because you are now *choosing* your stress battles. You recall your list of priorities, and you discover that, in the eternal scope of things, a toilet, dishwasher, and freezer aren't really worth *that* much stress. Anyway, they have been repaired. You are only out some money and a carton of chocolate ice cream. Becoming overly stressed would have cost you much more than that.

Everyday faith exercises:

(See #2, 3, 6, 7, 13, 29, 34, 36, 39, 43, 47, 50, 71, 72, 73, 75, and 82.)

Scriptural reminder of faith:

2 Corinthians 4:7-14: Even when we feel pressured on every side, we are not crushed. Christ keeps working in us, with us, even when the toilet, dishwasher, and freezer don't.

Life's Everyday Stressful Situation #7

"The older I become, the less work I can accomplish," a friend recently admitted. "I get so frustrated with myself because I can't do everything I used to be able to do."

We all feel this way at one time or another. For various reasons (that is, age, surgery, sickness), all of us must slow down from time to time. The frustration of having to slow down can cause considerable stress.

Everyday stress tells you to:

Push yourself. Don't let yourself slow down. There's work to be done, and you are the only one who can do it.

Everyday faith allows you to:

Be kind to yourself. Become your own best friend. Listen to what your body tells you. Give yourself the right to rest when you need to. If possible, hire someone to help you with your work load. Become more aware of your physical limits. We all have our physical limitations. Slow down, relax more, respect and be gentle with the body God gave you.

Everyday faith exercises:

(See #1, 2, 4, 5, 29, 30, 31, 32, 33, 34, 39, 40, 47, 50, 67, 68, 69, 72, 73, 74, 75, 76, 77, 82, 83, 85, and 90.)

Scriptural reminder of faith:

1 Corinthians 3:16: Be kind to your body and take care of it, for not only does it sustain your life; it is the temple of God's Spirit.

Life's Everyday Stressful Situation #8

You write out the month's bills, making only the allowed minimum payment on your credit cards, and you discover you have only $3.63 left in your checking account. Each month, it seems, more money goes out than comes in. With credit card interest rates piling up on you, you know next month's bills will be worse. You feel like pulling your hair out. You and your spouse are already both working hard at full-time jobs. A second job for either of you would be much too difficult. You don't know what to do.

Everyday stress tells you to:

Go ahead and pull your hair out. It'll ease your frustration. And, while you're at it, check out the local fast-food place. The sign in the window says they need some evening help. Maybe you could both take a second job—you know, just until you can make ends meet.

Everyday faith allows you to:

Forget the second job. Better to give yourself restful evening time, hours to celebrate your family, and some breathing room between jobs and activities. Instead of taking on more jobs, strive to reduce your financial stress. Why not sit down together and carefully assess your needs and purchases? Discover what you can live without and what purchases are really necessary. Ask yourself: Would I spend less money if I didn't have credit cards? Are my credit cards worth the extra monthly interest I have to pay? If credit cards prove to be a problem, cut them up and throw them away.

Seek to simplify your life-style and lower your expenses wherever, whenever you can. Pray together about the problems money has caused you, and ask God to guide you in your Christian consumerism. Seek outside financial counseling help if you need it.

Don't allow money to be the "master." It is your "servant" and not worthy of the stress it can cause you.

And, whatever you do, don't touch a hair on that beautiful head of yours!

Everyday faith exercises:

(See #1, 2, 3, 4, 5, 7, 10, 21, 33, 71, 72, 73, 75, 77, 78, 79, 80, 81, 82, 83, 85, 87, and 88.)

Scriptural reminder of faith:

Matthew 6:25-31: Even when we have only $3.63 in our checking accounts, we need not be anxious. We have a loving Father who has promised to watch over us, and, as hard as it can sometimes seem, we *can* trust Him to provide our everyday needs.

Life's Everyday Stressful Situation #9

You are bored. Just plain bored. All your days seem just alike: boring. Boring job, boring people, boring fast foods, boring housework, boring, boring, boring. Even the "seven-murders-a-minute" TV crime show is boring to you. You daydream about a cruise to the Bahamas, but it's boring to make reservations, buy traveler's checks, and pack clothes for the week. Anyway, you just don't have the energy for a cruise. You're in a stressful rut, and you don't know how to break out of it.

Everyday stress tells you:

"You're right. Life is a bore. Day after day, the same old stuff. It probably won't get any better either."

Everyday faith allows you to understand that:

The one sure way to end boredom is to reach out to others in Christ's love. Take inventory of your God-given skills and gifts, and then make a list of how you could use your gifts to help others. Begin to notice the needs around you. Set aside a time each day to telephone someone who is lonely, to drive someone who is disabled to a doctor's appointment, or to sit with someone who is sick. Find others in your church or community who also want to reach out. Then reach out together. You cannot reach out in Christ's love to others and remain bored. It's just not possible.

Everyday faith exercises:

(See #1, 2, 4, 5, 6, 7, 8, 9, 10, 11, 12, 21, 22, 24, 25, 26, 27, 28, 29, 30, 31, 32, 33, 34, 35, 36, 37, 38, 39, 40, 41, 42, 43, 44, 45, 46, 48, 49, 50, 51, 52, 53, 54, 55, 56, 57, 61, 62, 63, 64, 65, 66, 69, 70, 72, 73, 74, 75, 77, 83, 85, 87, 88, 90, 91, 92, 93, and 94.)

Scriptural reminder of faith:

Matthew 28:19-20: Go, and reach out to a hurting world with the message of Jesus Christ.

Life's Everyday Stressful Situation #10

You and your spouse are one of the 56 percent of America's two-paycheck families.[1] Your home is less like a "haven of rest" and more like a revolving door. You know no peace. Life seems a constant battle against time and energy. You and your children dress in a hurry to get to work and school on time. You grab fast-food breakfasts, lunches, and even dinners on the run. Business meetings, Scout activities, and piano lessons eat away almost every evening hour. You spend the weekends repairing broken shutters, grocery shopping for the next week, and buying shin guards for your son's upcoming soccer game.

You realize that your whole family is greatly stressed. You hope one day things will settle down a bit, but for now, you see no immediate change in the future.

Everyday stress tells you to:

Keep on keeping on. If 56 percent of Americans are living this life-style, then it must be the latest and greatest way to live. Anyway, the money's good, and you're able to give your kids all the things you didn't have when you were a kid.

Everyday faith allows you to:

Choose to call a halt to a life-style that offers little family time, no meaningful personal time, and constant daily stress on everybody. If you aren't pleased with your life-style, you can change it. It might mean, however, giving up some less important things for some more important things. Slowly, you can begin to incorporate meaningful personal and family activities into your day.

You might start by asking yourselves these questions: Could we share at least one meal a day as a family, even if someone must miss a business meeting or piano lesson? When could we set aside a few minutes a day to pray, worship, and read Scripture together? What activities could we plan as a family that would be most meaningful to us? Must we be so involved with work and school *after* work and school hours? Could we weed out some of the less meaningful individual activities in order to include more meaningful family activities? How could we make our home more of a restful "haven"? How would striving to develop a simpler life-style reduce our everyday stress and give us more family time together?

Everyday faith exercises:

(See #1, 2, 4, 6, 10, 13, 14, 15, 16, 17, 18, 19, 20, 29, 30, 33, 34, 36, 39, 43, 47, 48, 49, 50, 68, 72, 73, 74, 75, 76, 77, 78, 83, 85, 87, 88, 89, 90, and 91.)

Scriptural reminder of faith:

John 14: 16-18: So much faces us. So many tasks. So much to do in so little time. Too many people to care for, to please. Nowhere can we find rest and comfort. Does anyone understand? Can anyone hear? In a flash of a moment, God comes to us and reminds us of His promise: I will not leave you as orphans. I will come to you. I will be present in you. I will enable you.

God enables us to make changes in our lives. Putting God at the center of our lives is the most significant change we can make. In doing so, God gives us new insight and perspective into life. We also develop new priorities. With new insight, perspective, and priorities, we are better able to make life-changing and family-enriching changes.

Life's Everyday Stressful Situation #11

Morning freeway traffic is creeping. You're already seven minutes late to work when the cars in front of you come to a dead standstill: a car accident on the freeway. You know you'll be stuck in traffic for a while.

Everyday stress tells you to:

Say a few less-than-Christian words, blow your horn (that always relieves some stress), and bang your fists on the steering wheel. It'll make you feel better.

Everyday faith allows you to:

Accept the stressful situations you can't change or control. You're going to be late, and there's nothing you can do about that. So why not use the time productively?

How? Start by praying for the people involved in the car accident. Then lean back, close your eyes, and relax your body. Pray. Think about God; perhaps even mentally list all the words you can think of to describe God. Sing. Tell God you love Him and why. Repeat from memory your favorite Scripture verses. Count the blessings God has given you, and thank Him for them. Think about the ways you could reach out and minister to someone that day or week. Look out your window and notice with thanksgiving the beauty around you. Pray for the people who are stuck in traffic beside you (especially the ones who are blowing their horns and banging their fists on their steering wheels). All in all, allow this supposedly "unproductive" time to help you grow productively in your everyday faith.

Everyday faith exercises:

(See #1, 2, 3, 6, 7, 13, 14, 27, 33, 34, 35, 36, 38, 39, 40, 41, 43, 59, 61, 63, 69, 70, 71, 72, 73, and 83.)

Scriptural reminder of faith:

Psalm 9:1: David, the shepherd-boy-king, never had to contend with the morning freeway rush, but he, too, knew his share of stress. How did he deal with the stress of his day? The same way we can deal with the stress of our day.

"I will give thanks to the Lord with my whole heart; I will tell of all thy wonderful deeds. I will be glad and exult in thee, I will sing praise to thy name, O Most High."

Even when I'm stuck in traffic . . .

Life's Everyday Stressful Situation #12

You feel you have committed your greatest sin yet. You have hurt people you love, and you have hurt yourself. You feel sad, disappointed, and very guilty. You've prayed for forgiveness, but you don't feel forgiven. You feel too ashamed and embarrassed to admit your sin to those you've hurt. And you're not sure you could ever forgive yourself.

Everyday stress tells you to:

Struggle with your sin. Think about it all the time. Hate yourself, for anyone who could do THAT couldn't really be a faithful follower of Christ.

Everyday faith allows you to:

Confess your sin to God, repent of it, ask that He help you never to repeat it, and then seek His divine forgiveness. Asking God for courage, go to those you've hurt, and, in spite of the risk and embarrassment, confess and apologize.

Then ask God to help you to forgive yourself. You are human, and you've made a human mistake. You've been forgiven by God, you've asked for forgiveness from those you've hurt, and now you can forgive yourself. When and if you feel the sadness, disappointment, and guilt building again within you, take the situation back to God and leave it with Him. Find in Him peace for your soul.

Everyday faith exercises:

(See #2, 29, 30, 34, 50, 69, 70, 72, 76, 82, 83, 90, 96, 97, 98, 99, 100, and 101.)

Scriptural reminder of faith:

Colossians 1:13: "He has delivered us from the dominion of darkness and transferred us to the kingdom of his Beloved Son, in whom we have redemption, the forgiveness of sins."

Know that God has promised to forgive and to deliver us from the everyday stress of sin. Now, go in peace.

Note

1. A 1986 Bureau of Labor statistic.

Our time together has been brief. Much has been said, yet much has been left unsaid because of limited space.

We trust that our personal stories, our combined research, our faith exercises, and examples have been, and will continue to be, a practical help to you on your own journey away from everyday stress and into a deeper everyday faith.

That is our prayer for you.

* * *

May we leave you with our favorite blessing?

> The Lord bless you and keep you:
> The Lord make his face to shine upon you,
>   and be gracious to you:
> The Lord lift up his countenance upon you,
>   and give you peace. Amen.

Discussion Questions

1. Think about your own personal everyday stress. What bothers you most? Where do you feel most out of control? In which areas of your life do you feel most stressed? List the things that most stress you.

2. Think about your own personal everyday faith. Where are you the strongest in your faith? Where do you feel weakest? In which areas of your faith would you most like to grow?

3. List some of the most stressful situations you've faced. How did you handle them? In reflection, do you think you handled them well or poorly? If faced again with the same or a similar situation, what would you do now?

4. Reflecting upon those same stressful situations, think of ways you could handle stressful situations better by using examples of everyday faith.

5. Mentally, travel through an ordinary day. What common stressors do you encounter? Could you eliminate any of these stressors? If not, how could you better cope with them through practicing exercises of everyday faith? Do you believe your faith can make a difference in your daily and unavoidable stresses?

6. List the everyday faith exercises (from ch. 9) that you would like to incorporate into your day.

7. Write down what you discovered about yourself after taking the everyday stress test and everyday faith test.

8. Ponder these questions: How is your everyday faith as it is right now? What do you believe? How do your beliefs affect your everyday behavior?